THE SECRET IMPACTS

YOUR LIFE, THEIR STORIES

SARANYA E M

To the universe…

Disclaimer

This book contains narratives inspired by the author's personal experiences. Readers should be aware that memory is imperfect, and some gaps have been filled creatively in the book. While rooted in real events, these stories incorporate a few fictional elements to enhance narrative flow and artistic expression. Names, identities, locations, and certain details have been altered to protect privacy.

The author has made every effort to ensure accuracy, but these accounts reflect personal recollections and interpretations. They should not be considered definitive historical records. Any resemblance to actual persons, living or dead, or to actual events beyond those explicitly referenced, is entirely coincidental.

This work represents the author's perspective at the time of writing and is not intended as a comprehensive or objective account of the events portrayed. The author and publisher disclaim any liability for errors, omissions, or differing interpretations of the events described herein.

I Believe

The answers we seek are not far-flung but nestled in life's subtle signs—Just take a moment to pause, listen and unlock.

Contents

. . .

Author's Note

My Dear Reader,

Welcome to the world of stories!

To introduce myself, I am a person just like you; with dreams and disappointments, hopes and hurdles, facing challenges but learning from them and living a lot more every day. My name is Saranya and I appear as Sara throughout the book. As you turn each page, I assure you that I am right there sitting beside you, as a fellow companion, navigating the twists and turns happening in every story.

"The Secret Impacts" is my debut book, a collection of real-life stories inspired by people who have crossed my path and created a deep impact in my life. I started writing this book when I realised that it would be unfair to keep those lessons to myself; they are meant to be shared. Hence, I am passing them on to you.

Let me also give you a sneak peek here about the writing process, which is a story in itself.

Obviously, I began writing this book with a surge of energy and excitement. Each word was a journey back to those precious memories once again. But as time went on, the process became increasingly challenging and exhausting. Still, what kept me going was my husband's moral support and the deep connection I felt with those memories, making the journey both arduous and rewarding.

On top of that, from the beginning, I consciously kept my writing style simple and straightforward to ensure that you experience the same emotions as mine while meeting those extraordinary people. But let me share a secret with you: Simplicity is actually a complex craft. Trying to bring out a simple tone and a fast-paced narrative while staying true to the essence of the stories was like a delicate dance I learned, step by step, writing each and every word.

I remember times when I used to shut the doors and scream out loud, particularly when the book was in its middle phase. It demanded not just my time and energy, but also a piece of my soul. But now the good news is, after countless hours and numerous drafts, I successfully delivered my first baby and handed it over to you—The most awaited and meaningful moment of my life.

Having said that, what's the takeaway from this book? I promise you, as the last page turns, you will find that you haven't just read a book but relived your own stories; your very own version of it. Perhaps you will gain a fresh perspective on approaching life's challenges and finding joy in the small moments that are happening in your life.

Thank you for choosing to be on this journey with me. I hope you enjoy reading this book as much as I enjoyed spending moments with all those characters.

Happy reading...!!!

With love,

Sara

You're always welcome…

1

Guests Are Gods in India

If I remember correctly, I was just nine years old when Marimuthu came to our house for the first time. "I heard from the villagers that you have a big Jamun tree at your house," Marimuthu enquired our father. "Yes, we do have one," our father acknowledged.

"Would you consider leasing the tree to me until the season ends, *Anna*?" With hopeful eyes, Marimuthu proposed to our father.

Marimuthu was a poor middleman, a broker, who took trees for lease in nearby villages and supplied fruits to the vendors in town. His income wasn't a fixed one, in fact, it was determined by the quality of the fruits he supplied.

Since our father didn't know Marimuthu before and hadn't considered leasing the tree, he found himself in a dilemma for a while when Marimuthu came up with a sudden proposal. However, after a lengthy conversation, Marimuthu succeeded in convincing him and obtained the tree for that season. Then the very next day of their agreement, Marimuthu came to tie a green-coloured harvest net beneath the tree and went home.

Following that, every morning, Marimuthu would arrive at the tree with his tools, rest for a few minutes in the tree's shadow and start picking the ripened jamuns. Sometimes later, our mother would offer him *masala tea* and some snacks. Then he would collect the harvest and return to town to give it to the sellers.

The jamun tree had been in our house for many years. I still have memories of playing around the tree with our cousins, friends, and sometimes parents too. We would climb up the tree and pick fresh jamuns to eat. So, to be honest, initially, I didn't like Marimuthu when he was taking the juicy fruits away from us. But as time went on, I was the one who got more attached to him because he always made me laugh and I felt so happy around him. He was such a jovial person.

Whenever he visited the house, I would get so excited and leave everything to assist him, be it holding the ladder or loading fruits into a bullock cart. Not just me, with the passing days, even Marimuthu got attached to our family members and very soon he became one among us.

That was the period when people in towns and cities started preferring natural and chemical-free items, which eventually increased the demand for jamun fruit and its products. As a result, Marimuthu started getting a better-than-usual response from the vendors. He made good money in that season.

However, the season ended in the blink of an eye. It was then painful and hard to accept that we wouldn't be able to spend time with Marimuthu when he said that it was time for him to leave and take all of his equipment from our house. "I'll be missing your jokes, Mari Anna," I told him crying.

Marimuthu also got teary-eyed and was equally moved as he sensed my disheartening feeling. He put his hand on my head saying, "Please don't cry, *Kannu*. I will keep meeting you." Then he took a pause and sat beside me, offering more words of comfort. While leaving, he invited all of us to his house for the upcoming weekend.

Other than Marimuthu, we didn't know anyone in his house. So our father and mother politely turned down his invitation, not wanting to be a burden to his family. In fact, they added that Marimuthu can come to our house anytime here afterwards. However, he didn't accept their refusal. "I will be waiting for your arrival, you all must come," he gave us a kind command and left with his belongings.

• • •

Marimuthu's kindness and love was something that couldn't be ignored. It was a Saturday evening, and we all planned to go to his house. Our mother packed three varieties of succulent fruits and homemade sweets made up of ghee for his family and we set off from our house with a lot of excitement.

Marimuthu's village was ten miles away from our place. The entire stretch on either side was lined with farmlands that went on as far as our eyes could see. All the way down, it was truly fascinating to see women carrying hay on their heads, tractors busy with loading and unloading sugarcane, and various sounds of fields from a distance. We were thoroughly enjoying all of it; especially the therapeutic smell of freshly prepared brown sugar.

Though we came from the village, my brother Sarna and I were so small and we were not familiar with farm life. We spent most of the time in our house and never socialised, hence, seeing all those activities, we became curious and kept asking a lot of questions like how sugarcane was being cultivated, how rice was grown, and countless other queries that bubbled up within us. Our father patiently stopped the two-wheeler in front of each field to explain and clear our doubts. Although we had learnt a lot at each stop, none of us anticipated that our two-wheeler would break down soon.

"What are we gonna do now?" our mother exclaimed. Being unanswerable to her, our father also started worrying as it was slowly getting darker.

Back then, mobile phones were not as common among the general public as they are today. It was 8 pm when we got stuck in the middle of the pitch-dark field. The area was full of farmland, stretching endlessly under the night sky, with rows of crops swaying in the breeze. There was not even a single house. Still, our father tried to seek help, but in villages, life typically slowed down after sunset, thus the streets were empty. Having no other options, our father started pushing the two-wheeler and we all followed him, relying on his lead.

Just within two miles, my brother and I grew tired and completely worn out. Seeing the exhaustion on our faces, our parents carried both of us on their shoulders and continued walking, looking for help.

Luckily, within a few steps, they got hope—a small house near a Muneeswarar temple. Our parents quickly woke us up, "Get up both of you, we saw a house…", and we crossed the road to knock on the door.

I was barely awake when we stood in front of that random house. Our parents were hesitant to knock on the door for obvious reasons. I was also worried that our arrival would be a disturbance to them, but to my surprise, the people in the house greeted us with a warm smile. "*Vanga, vanga!* How do you do?" a middle-aged couple opened the door and these were their first words for strangers like us.

Before our parents could say anything, understanding our situation, the couple gave us a spot near their bullock cart to park our two-wheeler and asked us to come inside. Truly, their kind gesture made us feel like they already knew us.

. . .

It was a beautiful thatched house with only one room. The floor was traditionally smeared with cow dung, giving off an earthy smell. The kitchen was neatly separated with a small divider and they also had a backyard where they grew their everyday vegetables.

As our eyes moved around the house, we realised that people there had been sleeping and they woke up as we arrived. The couple had four children who quickly cleared the space, moving their sleeping mats and pillows for us to sit.

Perceiving all those things, our father, feeling a little embarrassed, apologised, saying, "We're sorry that we woke you up."

But they were so kind, they didn't see us as a disturbance and immediately dismissed our father's concern. "Absolutely not," they said and offered each one of us a tumbler of pot water. Following that they served a hot cup of tea to our parents and *laddus*, a round Indian sweet, for me and my brother.

"Where are you coming from?" The man of the house started the conversation. Our parents replied to him and asked what work he did. "We've been farmers for the past five generations, and have a sugarcane field a mile from here," he replied. Then the heartwarming conversations continued for a long time as if we all were close relatives.

In the meantime, their four children went to the backyard to cut banana leaves for our dinner while the woman had already started preparing food for us. It was truly embarrassing for us to see them put in so much effort for strangers.

Seeing their kindness, our mother, with a heavy heart, quietly made her way to the kitchen and informed the woman that we needed to leave.

As we departed, our parents expressed gratitude towards the kind family with a heartfelt gesture of folded hands and said, "Thank you so much for your help, we will come back with a mechanic tomorrow to collect the two-wheeler."

Turning to my brother and me, he asked us to greet them goodbye and express gratitude for their timely help. But the kind couple were upset that we didn't have dinner at their house and were concerned about us leaving in darkness. However, our parents had conveyed our appreciation for their hospitality and explained that Marimuthu was expecting us.

In India, it is believed that anyone who comes to our house should not leave empty-handed. So, they let us leave with a bag of jaggery and two mufflers for me and my brother. The man of the house and his eldest son walked us to the end of the street and showed us the directions to Marimuthu's village. We acknowledged their help once again and waved our hands in farewell, saying *"poyittu varom"*, meaning we would go for now and come back.

We left with a heavy heart but with a feeling of warmth from the strangers. On the whole, we stayed in the thatched house for just half an hour but during the course of time they took good care of us and double-checked often whether we were comfortable sitting there or not, which I could never forget.

"Without this family, I can't imagine how we would have managed with the kids on the road. They were such selfless and kind-hearted people," shared our mother, her voice filled with genuine appreciation. "That's the beauty of human connection, Selvi," our father responded.

· · ·

Since we were late, Marimuthu and his wife were waiting in front of their house. They were happy as they saw us approaching from a distance. "*Vanga, vanga!* How are you all?" Rasathi shouted from her place, "You took so long to reach our house." She was so concerned, she kept on asking questions and as we went closer to their house, Rasathi asked, "Was everything fine on your way?"

"We are all doing good," we replied while also narrating the little incident that caught us up on the way. We never saw Marimuthu's wife, Rasathi, but the brimming joy on her face took away all our weariness and hesitation which crept in due to the delay.

Their daughters, Ragini and Padmini, ran to us excitedly. Ragini carried our bags and Padmini took my little brother on her hip. Meanwhile, Marimuthu expressed his happiness about having us at his place and gestured to move inside.

Marimuthu rolled out a traditional grass mat to sit on, and like the woman in the thatched house, Rasathi welcomed us with pot water.

After talking for a while she hurried to the kitchen and brought the dinner items she had prepared for us to the centre of the house. We all felt so guilty that they had waited for us for so long without having their dinner until we arrived.

Ragini kept a pinch of salt in a corner of a banana leaf. Padmini served us a delicious sweet, *Mysore Pak*, rice, curry, and side dishes were served by Rasathi and we started eating.

"Is it too spicy?" Rasathi asked our mother.

"Oh no! Not at all, it's tastier than I make," our mother complimented Rasathi and asked all of them to sit down with us for dinner.

"No, no, guests should eat first," Marimuthu replied with a smile. Though we wanted them to eat with us, we also respected their emotions, hence, continued eating.

The dinner was incredibly tasty and once we finished eating, Marimuthu and his wife gathered the banana leaves in which we ate. "We will dispose of it; you go wash your hands in the backyard," Rasathi directed us.

After washing our hands, our mother served dinner for Marimuthu's family and at last we all went to *thinnai*, a raised platform in front of the house to have a chit-chat under the moonlight. Meanwhile, Ragini and Padmini came up with betel leaves and betel nuts on a small plate for our parents.

It was an unforgettable experience for me to sit with Marimuthu's family and listen to their engaging stories. Interestingly, amidst the lively conversation, Marimuthu told us about a temple festival going on in their village and he wanted to take us to the temple the next day. We all were so excited hearing him and quickly went to sleep.

Marimuthu selflessly offered his sleeping space to our father; on the other hand, Rasathi and her daughters shared their bedsheets and pillows with our mother and us, ensuring everyone had a comfortable and cosy place to rest for the night.

The next morning, Rasathi and Marimuthu woke up early and arranged hot water for our bath. After having our wholesome breakfast, we set off for the village festival, the one Marimuthu had spoken about the previous night. True to his words, it was indeed a grand celebration. Devotees from surrounding villages gathered to partake in the festivities and to pull the temple chariot of the goddess.

It was indeed so good to witness the majestic chariot, slowly moving through the village streets carrying God's idol. We also joined the massive procession and afterwards, went inside the temple to offer prayers to the deity. Although it took us over three hours to navigate through the crowd and catch a glimpse of the goddess, the overall experience was nothing short of magical.

Once our temple visit was over, we finally planned to leave Marimuthu's village.

From the vibrant festive shops, Rasathi and Marimuthu picked up toys for me and my brother, along with some memorable gifts that they could afford.

"We will be looking forward to seeing you all at the next festival also," Rasathi's voice cracked with emotion as she told our mother.

"Of course. You should also come to our house," our mother too extended a heartfelt invitation.

In just a single night, our mother became quite attached to Rasathi and likewise, I and my brother with their daughters, Ragini and Padmini.

It was difficult for all of us to leave, and with a heavy heart we said, "*poyittu varom*".

"We will miss you," said Ragini and Padmini. And in a gesture of love and affection, Ragini quickly removed her green glass bangle that she wore and gave it to me, "Keep this…," she said. "Thank you so much for your love Ragini *Akka*. I'll treasure this precious bangle and will keep it close to my heart forever," I told her with lots of love.

Saying this, we headed to the thatched house to collect our two-wheeler with a mechanic.

While returning to our home through the same sugarcane field, I found myself taken aback by the hospitality and warm reception of both families. They had a genuine smile on their face and they truly treated us with the utmost respect and compassion.

Recalling our conversations and the beautiful time spent with the family, I asked our father, "*Appa*, why were both the families so welcoming and treated us like royalty, when they could have easily ignored us?"

"Because in India, we treat guests as gods," he responded with pride. Also, he subtly gave me and my brother a lesson for life that, no matter whether it is a planned or unplanned visit, guests should always be treated as gods and welcomed with open hearts.

We nodded in agreement as his words deeply impacted us that day.

• • •

"We will not be at home until 4 pm, please come after that," I received a text message recently.

Vasan and Vanitha were a lovely couple. Though Vasan was my husband's friend, we also shared a deeper connection with his family. They used to come to our house quite often for night stays and it almost became a tradition for us.

Whenever we heard they were on the way, I would excitedly prepare special dishes for them. Those visits were then filled with laughter, we would spend our nights watching family movies; and our days playing various games, creating memorable moments.

Every time Vasan and Vanitha left, they would invite us to their house but we kept on postponing as we couldn't find the right time.

Finally, one January, we decided to visit Vasan's house. They said they were thrilled when they heard from us.

Like our mother, I also prepared ghee sweets, picked up different varieties of fruits and went to Vasan's house with a lot of excitement. It was a 30 km ride from our place. However, unlike our journey to Marimuthu's house, there were no women carrying hay, no tractors loading and unloading, and no lush greenery in sight. Instead, there were tall buildings on either side of the road, people were dressed in neat and cosy outfits, some briskly walking with laptops on their backs and others with mobile phones glued to their ears. Seeing all those things, within a mile, I found the scenery monotonous and it failed to hold my interest. So, I ended up dozing off.

Only after reaching our destination did we realise that we weren't given the exact address of Vasan's house. "I thought he sent a message to you," I told my husband but soon realised that he also assumed that Vasan gave me the address, and from that very moment, the struggle began. Anyhow, to our dismay, Vasan didn't pick up our call or call us back for more than twenty minutes.

"Vasan, could you please send us the name of your apartment and the floor number?" We texted him twice standing on a random street corner.

"Search for Aishwarya Apartments, it's one of the biggest around here," Vasan texted back. Yet, he didn't provide us with the complete address even now. "Excuse me, could you tell me where Aishwarya Apartment is?" I asked a nearby shopkeeper.

"Are you referring to the newer one or the old one?" The shopkeeper confused me.

"The newer one," Vasan briefly responded after two more calls.

"Lift lobby C, floor number 09 and unit number 450," everything was pulled from Vasan after a series of phone calls and messages. The disappointing part was that Vasan never apologised for missing our phone calls or making us wait. Nevertheless, we pacified ourselves by assuming that Vasan must be busy.

After a bit of struggle, we finally arrived at Vasan's house. Despite the door being half-open, we rang the bell. "Tell them I'm sleeping," Vanitha said to Vasan, not realising we could hear her from outside. It was a jarring and hurtful moment to know that our friend said those words, but we kept our reactions to ourselves when Vasan came to the entrance.

By this time, we didn't even feel like going inside but everything was happening so fast for us to register and take action. Also, both of us have calm and composed personalities, hence we kept ignoring their unacceptable behaviour.

When he saw us, Vasan acknowledged our presence with a nod. We then greeted him, asking, "How do you do?"

"Yeah, good," he responded uninterestedly.

A couch was shown to us to sit on and Vasan inquired about our journey. I began to answer, "Yes, it was goo…" but my response was abruptly interrupted as he quickly moved on to the next formal question, turning to my husband, "How is your work going?" The lack of interest in our visit was evident in Vasan's behaviour, and his actions continued to confirm it.

We had known Vasan for a long time, he was a big chatterbox. Whenever Vasan's family visited our home, Vasan and Vanitha would freely move around the bedroom, kitchen, and guest room as if they owned the place. However, that day, we encountered a different Vasan, his attitude seemed off and utterly strange to us. It made us feel awkward being there.

"Can I get some water?" I was really thirsty and I don't think he would offer without asking.

"Sure," Vasan walked into the kitchen.

As he left, I couldn't ignore the feeling that something was amiss. "Maybe they have some family issues and we came at the wrong time," I said to my husband. "I don't think so. They knew about our visit in advance and they could have ignored it or maybe clearly told us. Besides, Vasan and Vanitha were talking normally while we stood out," he reasoned.

"Have it please," Vasan came with a glass of chilled water.

"Where are the children?" I asked.

"They are yet to return from swimming class," Vasan replied.

It felt like Vasan was trying hard to pretend that everything was normal but the drama was ruined within a second, "Hello, Aunty!" Mitra, Vasan's ten-year-old daughter, ran out from the master bedroom and hopped onto my lap. "Oops, I totally forgot that she came. See I'm getting older now," Vasan tried to manage with a silly excuse.

However, from the moment she came, Mitra was scanning something around and trying to figure out if we were planning to stay at their house or not. I quickly caught on to what she was up to. So I slowly slid our duffle bag under the couch and gave her a hint that we wouldn't be staying long.

Mitra, without wasting any time, hurried to the master bedroom to pass the news to Vanitha. "Though the informer was younger, she executed Vanitha's request seamlessly," my husband and I silently acknowledged each other. Then after a brief chat, Vasan also disappeared into the master bedroom, leaving us all alone in their living room and didn't return.

I generally take a long time to understand people's bad conduct but my husband was a quick learner. "It seems like their invite was merely a formality. Without knowing that, we came with clothes for the night stay," he remarked, feeling hurt.

"Let's go then," I immediately told my husband to preserve our self-respect. "It's embarrassing to sit in someone's living room alone when they were evidently waiting for us to leave," I added with disappointment.

We then picked up our phone and called Vasan from the living room. "It's time for us, Vasan, we want to leave now," my husband said, trying not to sound disappointed.

"Oh, just a sec, I'm coming," Vasan replied, stepping out of the bedroom with his regular pretentious smiling face.

"Ah! You people are disappointing us, we thought you'd leave tomorrow afternoon," Vasan said as he was upset. Vanitha and her younger son also came into the living room. "You should come home again," she said, putting on a show.

"For sure," we agreed, as we didn't want to offend them.

We stepped outside, took our slippers and turned to bid farewell, saying, "*poyittu varom*," but Vanitha and Vasan had already shut the door. Obviously, it was painful for us, especially after realising that the couple were only takers, not givers.

They already disrespected us, but the closed door stood as a strong proof of their lack of affection for us. Vasan and Vanitha were tremendously rude. They not only shut the door that day but drew a line between us and the bond we shared. And it was a pang of disappointment, realising that the heartfelt emotions we had, were one-sided.

This whole incident teleported me back to my childhood. "Those days people had a ready smile when they saw guests coming to their houses but now these people only smile when guests leave," I told my husband, being disheartened and narrating my journey to Marimuthu's house while we were returning from Vasan's place.

"Seems like Guests are no longer treated as Gods now, doesn't it?" he remarked.

When we were travelling back, though I was physically sitting next to my husband, I was lost in my thoughts of how Vasan and Vanitha mistreated us. I literally couldn't accept the reality that the culture I admired once, was changing in front of my eyes. But my husband tried his best to lift my spirits, "How about we grab some *falooda* or *bubble tea* on our way?"

I smiled at him and so, we headed home trying to forget the disappointing experience we had.

. . .

The very next week, Vasan and Vanitha came to our house for an overnight stay, pretending as if nothing had happened. However, despite their ill-mannered behaviour, my husband and I remained as Marimuthu and Rasathi when those guests came to our house—For us, *Atithi Devo Bhava* still stands true.

The Clash…

2

The Tight Slap

It was our first day of college. I was super excited and nervous at the same time. The classroom was really big, filled with students from varied states and districts. As an introvert, I was reluctant to strike up a conversation with anyone. That's when Radha, a petite girl with enchanting curls noticed my hesitation and took the initiation. In no time, we clicked and became good friends.

The classes commenced sharply at 9 a.m. Unlike schools, professors were friendly and approachable. They made it clear that there is no need to stand up and greet "Good Morning" and "Thank you" aloud every time as we did in school. They also insisted that we are grownups now and should act like one.

Since it was the first day, none of them bothered to cover the syllabus, instead, we had get-to-know-you sessions each hour. Although many of the students felt shy about introducing themselves, saying "My name is… and I'm coming from…", a few found the experience enjoyable. Moreover, the sessions were really engaging and helped us relax too. I also began to open up and feel more comfortable sharing about myself.

There was a free period in the second half of the day. By that time, we learnt a bit about each other and started to mingle with everyone except—Dhruv Mahadev. A short statured boy with an innocent and naive face. Though he was silently sitting in a corner his vulnerable nature made him an easy target for the boisterous students.

"Hey everyone, look at him! He's got a pencil box, just like a primary school kid," one of the mean students said, pointing at Dhruv when he was arranging stationery on his desk. The others laughed loudly, agreeing with the guy, "Yeah, funny right? I bet this school kid wouldn't even dare to say 'hi' to a girl! Such a scared-cat."

Hearing those hurtful comments, Dhruv's shoulders drooped and his eyes glued to the floor but the boys didn't stop humiliating him. Instead, they took advantage of the free period to bully him.

Radha and I felt sorry for him and we could never understand what that poor guy did to those boys to hear such mean comments. We managed to divert our attention by observing other students in the class, but we were suddenly interrupted by a staff member from the admin department. "Students! Come and collect your identity cards." He urged us to collect our cards at the earliest.

Upon hearing him, we all immediately made a beeline for the main building, at least Dhruv would be a bit relaxed now.

• • •

Out of nowhere, a guy named Sudhakar, joined me and Radha while we were collecting the cards. Though Sudhakar was the first one to get his card, he waited for us to join back and started to blabber something as he didn't know what to talk about. First of all, we have no idea why he joined us, and secondly, his pointless conversation didn't sit well with us.

"Sudhakar seems to be an attention seeker, doesn't he?" Radha whispered to me.

"*Ama!* How annoying!" I acknowledged Radha.

On top of that, once we returned to the class, Sudhakar took a seat next to us and continued to boast about his family's wealth and background. He didn't even care if Radha and I were comfortable listening to him or not. Eventually, when his chatter became too much to bear, we stopped responding. Sudhakar, getting the hint from us, cleared his spot and started goofing around the classroom.

A few minutes later, when he had no one to show off, he went straight to the class entrance and started scratching something on the door. Anyhow, Radha and I didn't truly mind him because we were busy exchanging stories about our school lives.

Sometime later, the remaining students started to show up one by one. Some laughed at Sudhakar and came inside, while others stood still as if he was the great artist Da Vinci. After all, he wanted that attention, especially from girls. So Sudhakar carried on with his showy acts.

At one point Sudhakar got so lost in impressing girls that he didn't notice a tall man coming to our classroom in a hurry—it was our Physics professor, Mr. Sethupathi. He already looked like a serious man and in no time we got its proof. He came to Sudhakar and ended his show with a tight slap.

The moment Sudhakar was ruthlessly slapped, students who were previously scattered around him, quickly got into the classroom and took their seats. The classroom that was filled with noise and chaos, transformed into a disciplined army, each one awaiting the next command in the fear of Sethu Sir. He was visibly irritated seeing Sudhakar's absurdity. "Idiot, don't you have the sense to put scratches on wooden doors?" his words cut through the silence.

"Sorry, sir," said Sudhakar, rubbing his cheeks.

"Keep your sorry to yourself." Then suddenly, Sethu Sir's eyes went to the words scratched on the door—"Sudhakar the Legend". Though the silly work made all of us laugh, it ended up making Sethu Sir even more angry. "Oh, are you a legend now? First, behave like a human, then think about becoming a legend."

"Senseless idiot…" Sethu Sir came into the class murmuring after shouting at Sudhakar.

Altogether, Sethu Sir was different from the other professors we met till now, he had a commanding and authoritative presence. He didn't let Sudhakar enter the classroom, "Clear the mess and enter my class, otherwise don't," Sethu Sir rebuked.

The scratches were quite deep though and didn't look like it could be removed.

Unlike other periods, there was no icebreaker. As soon as Sethu Sir entered the class, he started covering the syllabus giving a minute's introduction about him and how students should behave in his class.

None of us liked Sethu Sir and his dictatorship. However, the moment he started taking the class, we were all stunned. He was an excellent teacher. Despite his harshness, his unparalleled knowledge and dedication were truly remarkable. Moreover, he was the one who gave us confidence that Physics was not a complicated subject. He also encouraged us to ask questions anytime in the class or staffroom.

Finally, the class was over and Sethu Sir was about to leave. Meanwhile, Malar got up slowly from her seat and walked towards him, carrying a box of chocolates. She offered them to him with a smiling face, "Please take it, Sir". To our surprise, Sethu Sir neither wished her nor accepted the chocolates. Instead, he responded rudely, "I don't want your chocolates, get them out of my sight now." Frankly speaking, the response was on her face.

Malar, feeling utterly humiliated, went back to her seat putting her head down in shame. "He should have at least wished her," Radha said. Though we knew Sethu Sir was a tough person, his disgraceful behaviour was beyond our expectations. And we couldn't believe how someone could be so inconsiderate to a person who was simply sharing her birthday joy.

"Class dismissed. Don't forget your assignments tomorrow," Sethu Sir announced before walking out of the room, leaving behind a stunned silence. Despite publicly humiliating Malar, he seemed unaffected by it. Furthermore, it was clear that he knew he had deeply hurt her.

Not only Malar, as the first year of college came to an end, Rahul, Rathi, Kruba, and everyone including me were disheartened by Sethu Sir's cold behaviour on our birthdays. At first, we assumed he didn't like chocolate or perhaps he was diabetic. However, we eventually discovered that he liked sweets, but not those given on birthdays. On top of that, some of the seniors also told us that he wouldn't take birthday chocolates and warned us to be careful in his class. But we never lost hope and kept on trying our best to give him chocolates; and Sethu Sir? He kept on hurting us.

• • •

Days and months passed. We had come to the last few days of our first year and we were all immersed in preparing for our semester exams. Amidst the stress and the study sessions, there remained one more birthday to be celebrated in our class—Dhruv Mahadev's.

Dhruv was known for his quiet nature. Months turned into a year but he remained the same, and the group of bullies also didn't stop intimidating him. They used to trick him, fool him, and embarrass him in front of everyone to show off their false heroism. However, I don't remember Dhruv ever answering back. He always remained a silent sufferer.

Despite Dhruv being a brilliant student, his silence made him seem like a weak person in the classroom. It wasn't just the bullies; knowingly or unknowingly we all disregarded him. Consequently, no one considered him in any of the decisions taken in the class. He was treated as nothing more than a piece of furniture. When I look back now, I deeply regret it with a sense of guilt.

Since Dhruv's birthday was the last in our class, we couldn't help but wonder how Sethu Sir would react this time. Dhruv decided to discontinue his studies due to some personal reasons. Interestingly his birthday coincided with his last day in college.

Would Sethu Sir refuse Dhruv's birthday chocolates as usual or make an exception for him? The topic sparked lively discussion among us and curiosity about what would happen increased.

Though some of us speculated that Sethu Sir might show some leniency, considering his farewell, most of us were sure that Dhruv was not strong enough to tolerate Sethu Sir's usual harshness. So, being worried about Sethu Sir's behaviour towards birthdays, we suggested Dhruv to stay away from Sir.

But despite our endless attempts, Dhruv did not accept our suggestion. He generously bought chocolates for everyone—professors, students, lab technicians, security guards, and sanitary workers. All of them wished him wholeheartedly on his birthday but as the eighth hour was arriving, our curiosity peaked. We all were waiting for Sethu Sir to enter the class. I remember we had a class test on that day.

Dhruv patiently waited until the test was over. Once we finished and gave our test papers to Sethu Sir, Dhruv stood up and approached him with a box of chocolates.

"That's it, Sethu Sir is going to grill him today," a group of girls behind me murmured.

"Sethu Sir won't take Dhruv's last day of college as an excuse," one of the girls in that group kept her view strongly.

Moreover, Sethu Sir was in a sour mood that day, and as expected, Dhruv was severely embarrassed by him. But instead of returning to his seat in shame, as we did on our birthdays, Dhruv stepped forward courteously.

"I said, I don't take chocolates. Don't you understand that?" Sethu Sir responded harshly.

"I did, Sir."

"Then go back to your seat," said Sethu Sir and started dictating the assignments to all of us. But Dhruv was stubborn and refused to go back to his seat, even though he was asked to do so.

"It's my last day, Sir. You have hurt me with your words but I still want to ask—Why won't you accept our chocolates? What did we do?" Dhruv firmly questioned, standing his ground.

"What?!" We couldn't believe our ears. The boy who never spoke a word is standing in front of a person who is well-known for his discipline and quite infamous for turning harsh towards students on their birthdays, and not just standing but arguing with him.

For us, the clash looked like a silent challenge to Sethu Sir's authority.

"Idiot. Don't waste anyone's time here. If you stand here for one more minute, that idiot box will be thrown away," Sethu Sir's anger reached its peak and it was clear in his frequent usage of the word "idiot".

"He is going to get a tight slap anytime now," Sudhakar signalled to his friends from outside—who was known for repeating his blunders. Time and again, Sudhakar used to ignore the lessons learnt from his past mistakes, which always led to Sethu Sir punishing him and making him stand outside the class.

Anyhow, Dhruv persisted in asking the same question.

Hearing him repeat again and again, Sethu Sir eventually became furious and muttered, "You, irritating idiot…" Saying that he stepped down from his platform and approached Dhruv. Everyone present there, except Dhruv, was genuinely intimidated by Sethu Sir's aggressive walk.

"What do you think of yourself? You think you will become a hero if you question me like this?" Sethu Sir went even closer to Dhruv and his anger seemed out of the boundary.

However, Dhruv remained strong. "This is my last day in college," he said again. "Please tell us why you do not accept chocolates from us. I won't move until you answer us, Sir," Dhruv maintained a steady and calm pace.

"It's totally an unwanted trouble for Dhruv, especially on his last day," the boys discussed among themselves, even those bullies had concern for him now.

At last, we had only five minutes for the bell to ring but both Sethu Sir and Dhruv were adamant and tough to each other.

"Let's see what are we hearing first—the sound of the bell or cries of the poor boy?" I and Radha told each other nervously. However, as Dhruv raised his voice in demand once again, I quickly ducked down the table, not wanting to see him getting a tight slap.

• • •

"Five years ago, it was a student's birthday like you…" The unexpected shift in Sethu Sir's tone and the sudden storytelling caught my attention. I couldn't resist my curiosity and quickly rose from my hiding spot. Sethu Sir's eyes, usually stern, now seemed to hold a hint of reminiscence. The entire class went silent, eager to hear the story that had momentarily stayed the storm.

"Those days, I was not this tough but indeed a strict professor," Sethu Sir looked a bit hurtful when he started telling the story behind.

"Just like you all do, a student offered me a special chocolate. I wished him and blessed him with all my heart, and casually ate it in front of everyone. I didn't know that the birthday boy was waiting for me to finish the chocolate before he made a hurtful comment, which I will never forget. 'Free chocolate always tastes good, isn't it, Sir?' he shouted from the back bench and pretended as if he didn't do anything. But what shattered me the most was, that, the entire class erupted in laughter. Following him, some laughed louder, while others tried to stifle their giggles but not even a single student stood by me. What did I do to them other than give my best to teach them this subject? And the most painful part was, I was too late to realise that it was a planned effort to insult me. I can never forget that day. When I sat alone in the empty classroom afterwards, I questioned my worth as a teacher and vowed to regain my dignity. I wanted to ensure that such disrespect would never happen again. Hence, from that day forward, I decided to stop taking chocolates from students. I see it as a disgrace every time you people lift that idiot box in front of me," said Sethu Sir, leaving the whole class sad."

We all carried a pin-drop silence hearing Sethu Sir and it started hurting us when he asked, "Imagine how your father would feel if you insulted him in such a way. Isn't a guru more like a father?"

We nodded in affirmation.

"But I'm not the same boy, sir. Neither are my friends." Dhruv's response was straightforward and clear. He was not ready to take Sethu Sir's explanations as a justification for his actions.

"Dhruv has a point and he is clear," said Radha.

"We all love you, sir. Because of you, we got interested in Physics and scored well. Even though you were tough on us, we always came to you on our birthdays, hoping you would change. We are craving your soft corner, sir. Please understand that we are not the same person who insulted a guru five years ago. And I apologise on their behalf as well," saying that Dhruv turned to all of us to get up and say sorry. Understanding his signal, we all stood up and apologised to Sethu Sir for his past ordeal. "Forgive us and those students, sir. Please," we pleaded in unison.

Sethu Sir became speechless when he saw our love for him and readily accepted Dhruv's chocolate. Clearing his throat, Sethu Sir began to say something but the bell rang immediately. Normally, the bell would signal our eager escape from the classroom but that day, we ignored it completely and stayed put. Sethu Sir continued, his voice filled with emotion.

He asked all of us to sit down first. "Dhruv, I must thank you for being my teacher today," saying that Sethu Sir gave a pat on Dhruv's back. Sethu Sir then took a long pause and it seemed like he was trying to fetch words straight from his heart.

Until now, we had only seen Sethu Sir as a villain and we never grasped the emotions behind his stern facade. But for the first time in the whole year, I could piece together the significance of his previous actions.

No matter how many times a student went to him to solve doubts, he would always acknowledge it and make sure that we got the solution—the same way how our parents take care and wish for nothing but our betterment. The reason why we excelled in Physics was also because he desperately wanted us to understand the subject and not just learn for the sake of academics.

I realised, "Sethu Sir was more than a teacher; akin to our father. He just showed his love and care in his own way so far".

"I accept my faults," Sethu Sir resumed.

"I only saw the pain that I went through whenever my students approached me on their birthdays. I didn't realise that I was imparting the same pain on all of my students these many years. Dhruv, you are the first one who opened my eyes after the incident that happened 5 years back," said Sethu Sir.

That day, Sethu Sir's actions were a powerful teaching moment for us. It is so easy to argue and point out someone else's mistakes, but it requires an ego-free spirit and true modesty for a seasoned teacher to admit his own errors, especially in front of those who were not even as old as his professional experience.

And the highlight of the day was, we all had happy tears in our eyes when the genuine man, Sethu Sir, wished the whole class a belated birthday—"Happy birthday to all of you, my dear students."

Finally, Dhruv's sincere gesture on his birthday, coupled with Sethu Sir's unexpected response, transformed an ordinary day into a cherished and emotional experience that we would fondly reminisce about even for years to come.

As usual, Sethu Sir gave us the assignments and we started packing our bags to leave.

Sethu Sir left the class, staring at Sudhakar. "Sorry, Sudhakar. You will not be forgiven by him ever," we all burst into laughter seeing Sudhakar's confused face.

• • •

By the end of the day, we gave a small farewell to Dhruv and I still remember what I wrote in his scrapbook that day: "Dhruv, your absence will be felt…"

Then once the farewell was over, I returned to our college hostel and shared what happened when arrogance clashed with vulnerability. "Strength lies in silence," my roommate, Pooja, summed it up perfectly.

I was tasked…

3

Paati's Legacy

I was 12 years old when I accidentally met her—Swami Ammal—whom I affectionately call *Paati* (grandmother), now. The first time I saw her was quite unforgettable and it seemed as if the incident was predestined.

I was travelling in a public bus that day. Even though I was not interested in boarding it, imagining its crowd, I had no other choice. Usually, my father was the one who would drop and pick me up wherever I went. But that day, he was occupied with another task and, after a moment's hesitation, he instructed me to come on my own.

Buses were the most affordable and common mode of transport when I was younger. So I took a public bus, but to my annoyance, it was more congested than I anticipated; I was almost sandwiched among the people over there.

As soon as the bus departed from the stop, I saw an elderly woman trying to chase the bus, shouting and waving her hands to stop it.

It was Paati—a dark, thin and delicate woman, covered in sweat, and heavily breathing. "Why don't you find any other bus, Paati? You want to suffer here?" I mused and immediately urged the driver to stop the bus.

In places like my hometown, buses would often come late, and when they arrived, they were always crowded, just like the one I was in. Paati might not want to miss it and wait endlessly for the other one to arrive. So, despite the sea of people, she boarded the bus.

When Paati stepped in, it was truly disheartening to see her drenched in sweat. She tried her best to squeeze into the crowd and was having a tough time finding a spot to stand or even to take a breath. But despite her being an elderly woman and clearly struggling, no one, not even those in the priority seats, gave up their places for her; Paati didn't make any demands either.

Then after a few minutes of observing Paati's difficulty in finding space amidst the packed bus, a pregnant woman named Suja rose from her seat in a heartwarming gesture. "You can take my seat, Paati. I'll stand…" She was so kind to offer her seat, making way for Paati.

"*Vendam ma, ne utkaru*," Paati refused to take the seat as she noticed the woman was expecting. With a compassionate touch on Suja's shoulder, Paati insisted her to sit. This simple act of kindness sparked an instant connection between them, and soon, they were lost in conversation, creating a warm bubble amidst the bus's hustle and bustle. In fact, the best thing I liked about people at that time was the fact that they didn't hesitate to start up a conversation. Wherever they go, they get a feeling of belongingness; a sense of community and they make sure people around them also feel the same.

Likewise, Paati and Suja were expressive about their feelings. They had raw emotions without any filter—whether they were harsh or sweet.

"How many months now?" Paati initiated.

"Seven months, Paati," Suja replied. Subsequently, she asked where Paati was going.

"Where will I go other than my home?" Paati responded with a touch of humour, causing all of us to chuckle.

Now, as the conversation slowly unfolded, almost everyone around her, including me, was enveloped by Paati's warmth and joyous aura. She further told Suja that she runs a *rattai*, a wooden spinning wheel, at home, and comes to town once a week to sell yarn.

"It must be challenging for someone of her age," whispered a woman behind us after hearing Paati. "But look at her! She is telling it with such humour," another one expressed in awe.

Liking her magical ability to make people laugh instantly, a few other passengers also started to interact with Paati. However, amidst their conversation, Paati noticed my silence and the way I was watching them, "What's your name?" she asked. I immediately became overjoyed that I was also drawn into their circle.

I introduced myself and wanted to continue my conversation with Paati, but being a small girl, I didn't know how to proceed.

Even though it seemed silly, I asked, "How do you wear this *pin kosuvam* saree, Paati?" I really didn't mind people laughing at my question.

Pin kosuvam saree is one of the oldest styles of wearing saree in Tamil Nadu, where a small portion of pleats hangs at the back. I have always been intrigued by how effortlessly people wear it whenever I see them. So, I asked Paati.

First, she laughed out loud as other passengers and then roughly outlined how it should be hung at the back and the number of turns to take around the body. I then nodded in response to show her that I understood, even though I couldn't grasp the theoretical explanation she gave me.

"You look a lot like my second son's daughter, Kayal," Paati complimented me after her saree tutorial. Again, I was extremely happy to hear this from her, making me feel so special and close to her already.

"Oh, do you have two sons?" asked Suja.

"No, no," Paati corrected Suja, stating she had seven sons and one daughter. "Oh my god! Seven sons and a daughter…???" I wondered within myself.

"Then why would you want to suffer working at this age, Paati? Better rest at home," Suja asked with deep concern.

Hearing her words, Paati's expression changed abruptly, and she stopped laughing as if those words recalled a sad distant memory. "I always dreamt of dying while I work," Paati responded firmly, thinking we didn't notice the sudden shift in her expression. Further, her strong words clearly hinted at a deeper backstory to us than what she revealed.

By then, our bond with Paati had grown stronger, and we wanted to know the reason behind her pain. While some passengers were merely curious, and not genuinely compassionate, all were eager to uncover the reason behind her statement.

"Paati, if you don't mind, could you share a story with us?" Padma, who was standing beside me, asked with childlike curiosity.

"Why not? Once upon a time, Ram and Seetha…" Paati immediately began. "No, Paati, not that. We want to hear your story," Padma demanded, her request echoed by the rest of us. After all, that day, all the passengers around Paati proved that every adult harbours a child within, a child eager for stories and shared experiences from elders.

• • •

"I just attained puberty at that time…" Paati started.

"I got married to my aunt's son. He was a farmer who was eighteen years older than me. Though I came from a poor family, I was so happy and free until I lived with my parents. To my utter dismay, my life became hell when I entered my in-laws' house. They were so hard on me, and I was treated no less than an enslaved woman there. My husband however was a different person. He was caring and always stood by me." Paati's love and affection for her husband has never changed even after these many years and it was evident in her words.

She continued, "Soon my husband freed me from that hell as we moved out of the house. Then somehow, we managed to run the family with a small piece of land and had our children one after another. As time went by, I gave birth to our daughter Sharada after having seven sons.

It was the middle of the night. I was feeding my five-day-old baby when my husband had an attack. I didn't even know that my husband was dying. I was young and naive when he left us with all the burden on my shoulders. At that time, all this poor soul could do was cook and take care of my family. I didn't know anything beyond that—purchasing groceries, bargaining; I had no skills, no job, nothing. I had no idea how I would earn money thereafter. I was helpless, hopeless, and afraid of being in a lonely house in a remote village."

"Poor Paati," we all felt a deep sympathy for her and wondered how she moved ahead in life with eight children.

We then got to know from her that after her husband, she went to her brother's house to seek protection for herself and her children.

"I didn't go for money, yet we all were thrown out by my brother's wife as she assumed that this widow came to occupy her father's old house. That was never my intention, even when my husband was alive, we never conversed about the house. I couldn't see my children suffer, that's why I went there but God had other plans for me. At last, after bearing with all her harsh words, I pleaded for some food for my younger son as he was hungry and screaming. But she didn't help us. Instead, she warned all of us not to knock on their door ever again. My brother neither supported me nor controlled his wife. He just stood there, silently, while his wife treated me and my children like we were beggars," Paati welled up with tears as she reminisced about those days.

"How can a lady be so selfish and ruthless?" someone from the crowd said. "And especially one's own blood!!!" another voice exclaimed about her brother, while all of us were teary-eyed.

"That day, I made a solemn promise that I would never knock on anyone's door again," Paati continued. "I wanted to raise my children by myself and teach my brother's family that although I was a widow, I was not a beggar—I was a woman in need of moral support, not handouts.

Though I was downhearted, I returned to my home, stronger than before, and began taking on the responsibilities my husband had left behind. You know? Helplessness taught me a lot and made me realise how strong I was.

Initially, I faced many failures, but I persevered, sowing rice, running rattai, selling ghee, curd, and other dairy products, and doing whatever I could to feed my children. Most days, my eldest son and I went to bed hungry so that the rest of the children could eat. However, neither I stopped any of them from going to school nor I went back to my brother for help.

Time moved on; all my children had grown up and secured good jobs, but I kept working. When each one of them turned 25, I found a suitable girl and was determined to take over their wedding cost completely. After all, they were my children, and it was my responsibility to oversee their weddings, regardless of whether I had the financial capacity to do so or not. To fulfil this commitment, I had no other option but to sell my cattle, one by one, for each wedding, and I'm happy about that.

Then, I used to keep the newly married couples for 18 days in my home and sent them out with 5 kgs of rice, 3 varieties of lentils and a few groceries to start their own life. I wanted my children to live independently. It was seventeen years ago that I sold my last cattle for Sharada's wedding." Paati had a pleasant smile on her face and a sense of pride saying this. We also smiled with her as our hearts felt relaxed.

"Now, all my children are in a good position in society. Although I am a widow, I am proud that I have fulfilled the responsibilities my husband left on my shoulder," Paati finished her story and took a deep breath.

Everyone on the bus now was stunned by her story and stood there in awe of Paati.

"You are so inspiring, Paati," I said, getting emotional.

"Is there nobody to take care of you now?" Suja inquired of Paati after clearing her throat.

"I'm blessed to have such caring daughter-in-laws and grandchildren. They love me more than anything in this world. However, I have always chosen the path of self-reliance and have never knocked on anyone's door.

My children and their families visit my small house whenever they can. I cook with whatever I have, and we sit in a big circle to eat. My grandchildren help me run rattai, just as their parents used to do at their age, and we all sleep together. They never complain about a small house or limited food options. They love visiting me and have immense respect for me. My children raised them well and what else can give me happiness? I feel my life is complete now."

Both Suja and I were moved after learning about Paati's inspiring story and lifestyle. Although Paati had all the means to live in an air-conditioned room in her children's house, she chose to reject that. Instead, she lived in a small mud house, making ends meet with her limited income. "Paati was not just another face in the crowd; she was exceptional," Suja and I exchanged our expressions, reflecting a deep respect for Paati.

Suddenly, a jolt shook us—both physically and mentally. That was Paati's stop, and she was about to leave. It was so hard for Suja and me when we desperately wanted to continue our candid conversation with Paati. She felt like our very own grandma to us.

"Anyhow, Paati's story will always remain in our minds," we consoled ourselves looking sadly at each other.

Despite feeling upset, Paati blessed us both and went down, taking her age-old canvas bag. Suja and I immediately poked our heads out of the window to wave goodbye to Paati, but to our surprise, she was returning to the bus.

"Why is she returning…???" we asked ourselves confused and excited. Suja exclaimed that maybe Paati wanted to continue travelling with us. "No. She might have left her belongings in the bus, I guess," I replied to Suja. But both of us weren't right.

The moment Paati stepped back onto the bus, she quickly pulled her *surukku pai*, a drawstring pouch she kept at her right hip, and turned towards me. "Hold it tightly, *kannu*," she hurriedly handed me Rs.10 and left the bus as the driver was waiting to take off.

It was at that moment I realised that the conductor had forgotten to issue Paati a ticket amidst the chaos. I was surprised because no one had noticed this, and Paati could have easily saved her money instead of purchasing the ticket. But she didn't want to travel without paying her fare or cheat the conductor. Instead, she handed me almost thrice the money to buy her ticket.

Paati then waved goodbye to Suja and me as the bus slowly moved from her stop.

"*Ahhhhhn…ticket, vangu, ticket ticket,*" the conductor's voice rang out as he approached the front to issue tickets. I gave the money and bought a ticket for Paati.

• • •

Many times I feel like God has his own interesting ways for us to meet superhumans like Paati, to make us understand the nuances of life. That day, I could have missed meeting Paati if my father hadn't got that urgent work.

Knowingly or unknowingly Paati taught me a lesson for life. Though this incident happened years back, whenever I feel that my life struggles are way too much and unfair, I remember Paati with innate respect. Her story runs in my mind like a videotape and gives me the strength to move on.

But it was not just her hard work or determination that made Paati a superhuman to all of us; instead, I believe it was her integrity that came along with it; It was her humble and down-to-earth nature that made her stand out in that bus.

I often wonder, how many women like Swami Ammal, seemingly ordinary, do exist in every corner, every street, every bus stand, waving at us to impart their knowledge, come into our lives like magic, and heal us?

On that day, I got down at the next stop and I genuinely didn't know what to do with Paati's ticket or how to return her balance money. Yet, I told myself that it was given to me with a reason—I'm responsible for carrying forward Paati's legacy to the next generation.

And this is how villagers started respecting Krishna…

4

Krishna and His Kattil Kadai

Krishna, Kamala, Ram, and Lakshman were close friends studying in the eighth grade at the local school. Letting out sheep and chickens, tickling people sleeping on *thinnai*, banging random doors and snaffling farmlands were their everyday entertainment once they came from school.

Nobody in the village liked those cheeky children. But the mischief-makers never bothered being labelled as corn thieves, pranksters, and troublemakers by the villagers. They continued living their lives on their terms and enjoying it to the fullest.

Krishna's mother, Rajamma, worked in a nearby power loom unit. His father abandoned them when he was just two years old. Despite battling lung disease, Rajamma was a determined worker and served as both father and mother to Krishna. Ram and Lakshman were twin brothers. Their parents worked in the demanding profession of handloom saree weaving. Even though the job didn't provide well for the family, they continued doing so because it had been a generational tradition. The only girl in the group, Kamala, belonged to a well-settled family. Her mother was a homemaker, and her father was a pawnbroker. Her parents viewed everything through a financial lens and only socialised when there was a potential benefit. Obviously, they didn't like Kamala's friendship with the boys due to their family background and financial status. However, Kamala was a free-spirited girl who followed her heart without calculating the advantages as her parents did.

Since all four were studying in the same school, every morning they would gather at the old Murugan temple located at the centre of their village, and from there, they would walk to the school. Fearing that these naughty boys might skip school to play in the cornfields, Kamala would take charge to ensure the boys were attending school. Hence, every day Kamala would arrive an hour early, waiting on the temple steps for the boys to join her.

Most of the time, the boys would arrive late and leave their school bags lethargically with Kamala, before hurrying to Kasi's shop—a daily ritual they never skipped. Meanwhile, Kamala, ever so responsible, would complete their homework, knowing well the boys might not do it themselves.

Kasi was a wolfish guy. Though he was a grocer, his major income came from selling "Kid's Lucky Lottery". Priced at Rs. 1 each, Kasi's shop offered a special deal throughout the year— Free Unlimited Scratching. He encouraged children to scratch several cards for free for the whole week luring them with potential prizes. But there was a catch: By the end of the week, Kasi would collect the debts and an additional two rupees as an interest; making sure his gamble always paid off.

None of the parents liked their children visiting Kasi's shop for obvious reasons. So, the boys kept their lottery dealings a secret. They managed to fund their small venture by using money intended for exam fees, special fees, and whatever else they could make up in front of their parents.

Although Kamala tried to control the boys' addiction and told them about Kasi's cunningness, it was of no use. Instead, influenced by Kasi, they woke up every morning with a stupid goal: To win the "Mega Jackpot"—a five-hundred rupee note. But at that time the boys didn't know that their lives would take an unexpected turn, especially Krishna's.

• • •

It was the middle of the academic year, and the school announced the conduct of a half-yearly examination.

From Mathematics to Tamil, Kamala did so well in every subject but the boys seldom wrote for thirty minutes each day. Instead, they wasted their time staring at walls, taking restroom breaks, sneezing, yawning, and scratching the desk. Krishna was specifically the most mischievous one and ignored the fact that his mother was working hard to provide him with education.

On the last day of their exam, Kamala's parents came straight to the school to pick her up. Her grandmother was living in North India, and they used to go there twice a year.

Kamala was a very affectionate and caring girl. So, leaving the boys for the next fifteen days was really hard for her. But on the other hand, the boys were thrilled that their control system was getting turned off for the next few days. And as soon as Kamala left, they excitedly took the opportunity to have some fun and indulge in mischief.

Throughout the holiday their joy and trouble were in equal measure, much to the villagers' dismay—pranking, sneaking and irritating people. Moreover, their antics grew bolder with each passing day, sparking increasing annoyance among people.

Complaints soon started arriving at their doorsteps and their parents were fed up listening to the villagers. However, Rajamma, Krishna's mother, always stood by them as their unwavering defender.

For her, education was the key to the future, and as long as the boys were engaged in their studies, everything else was secondary. Rajamma saw the world through the eyes of those children so she excused their playful escapades. Hence the boys' mischief always got hidden behind Rajamma's love and they continued causing trouble to the villagers.

. . .

School reopened…

Kamala did not return to school due to her grandmother's illness. But taking it as an advantage, the boys became even more unruly and willful inside the class—paper aeroplanes took flight, desks turned into drum sets, teachers were mocked as soon as they turned to the blackboard, and weird animal-like noises filled the classroom.

Suddenly, after five days, while Rajamma was working at the power loom unit, Krishna's class teacher paid her a visit. Around that time, it wasn't uncommon for the school teachers to come home and have a word with parents. Sometimes they also came only to convince the parents to send their children to school explaining the importance of education. Hence child labour was largely reduced then. However, on that particular day, Krishna's teacher had a different agenda. She had visited to tell Rajamma to "stop sending Krishna to school" since he was spoiling other children in the classroom.

Rajamma was taken aback by the teacher's unexpected statement and didn't understand what was she talking about. "Dear *Teacher Amma*, I think you're mistaken and may be talking to the wrong parent. My son Krishna always scored well in school and he has been a good student. I don't understand, why should I stop him from going to school?" asked Rajamma with respect.

"Don't you know anything? Omg! Where have you been?" The teacher became upset when she noticed Rajamma's lack of awareness and showed Krishna's report card to her.

"What does it say, teacher Amma?" Rajamma inquired.

Since Rajamma was unschooled, it seemed Krishna easily cheated her whenever he got the report cards. Krishna had failed in all the examinations throughout the year, including the recent half-yearly, and he lied to Rajamma that he scored well.

"Not only that, Rajamma! Your son apparently won some kid's lottery today and used all the money to buy fresh scratch cards. We didn't know that Krishna was selling scratch cards in the classroom and spoiling others until one of the students informed us. The headmaster is shouting at me because of what your son did today."

"How come I am responsible for such a disobedient boy like yours? He acts like he is a big businessman and can do anything he wants to. I don't know who is teaching him all this. You surely look like an innocent lady, but how is it fair on my part to be blamed for your son's troublesome behaviour? You tell me that, Rajamma," the teacher questioned her angrily. Even though the teacher understood how Krishna fooled his mother and felt sorry for Rajamma, she couldn't control her anger.

Rajamma obviously had no answers to the teacher's endless questions.

At last, the teacher insisted sternly to Rajamma to keep her son at home and not send him to school anymore.

After hearing her, Rajamma didn't know what to do, she just stood there, speechless. The truth hit her hard, and she was stunned to realise how ignorant she was those many days. "So all these days…he wasn't studying?!" Rajamma couldn't accept when her trust in Krishna and expectations for his future had crumbled. Moreover, she was ashamed as the teacher revealed everything in front of all the labourers in the unit, particularly before those, who complained about the boys a few days ago. "Rajamma needs this," some of them murmured, finding satisfaction in her embarrassment. Some even went to the extent of relating Krishna's disobedience to his absconded father.

The villagers' harsh words brought tears to Rajamma, and as a consequence, her heart closed off to Krishna forever. Though these many days Rajamma had been working day in and day out to provide education for her one and only son Krishna, she now decided to stop sending him to school. She was not ready to accept any more complaints and insults. She also stopped talking to Krishna.

But despite being aware of his mother's anger, Krishna remained indifferent, assuming she would calm down in a week or so while maintaining his usual cool and lethargic demeanour. He didn't worry about not going to school. In fact, he was happy in his own world and this was actually freedom for him.

Every day, Krishna would wander around the village to pass the time uselessly until Ram and Lakshman returned from school so they could play together. Mostly they used to play around the temple and trouble people over there or at the familiar corner of Krishna's house.

One day, while playing at his house, the boys happened to discover a forgotten storage trunk. "What's this, Krishna?" Ram was curious to know what was inside the mysterious box. "I've never seen it before," Krishna replied and with a clever tap of a stone, they unlocked the box. But they didn't find anything interesting as they expected it was full of treasure or playthings. Instead, there was a bundle of old papers nestled among some shirts and dhotis. "Hey, these must be your father's," said Ram, lifting the clothes that seemed to have belonged to Krishna's father.

Krishna, who had never known much about his father, began to sift through the papers. His eyes raced across each and every line with an eager intensity. Ram and Lakshman also joined him, their heads close together as he read out.

"My father took a loan from someone a few years back???" asked Krishna, his voice tinged with confusion after reading a set of papers. Ram and Lakshman nodded in unison to acknowledge the shocking revelation.

"*Pavam*, Krishna. It seems, your mother has been tirelessly working to pay off these debts and hoping to give a better life to you. You mean everything to her," Lakshman said with empathy and a hint of sorrow.

Krishna was truly unaware of his father's debts before and was surprised to learn that their small house was also mortgaged. Now, he could relate to why his mother was working three shifts daily. And only then, Krishna realised the reality of how painful it must have been for Rajamma that day when she discovered her son was as irresponsible as her absconded husband. He also felt guilty for cheating his mother and for ignoring her health issues.

Krishna was disheartened by the truth, but this time, for good. Despite his young age, knowing about his mother's plight ignited a deep sense of responsibility within him, which was surprising for Ram and Lakshman.

That day, the young teen made a solemn vow to repay every penny and provide a better life for his mother—a vow that would become the bedrock of his determination and the axis around which their lives would turn. Truly, it was a moment of clarity and resolve, one that transformed Krishna from a carefree boy into a young man driven by purpose. And this promise marked the beginning of a journey that would shape their future.

"We will also help you with whatever you do to pay the loan, Krishna," said Ram and Lakshman, determined to stand by their friend. "But earning money, though—how do we do that?" Ram pondered aloud, scratching his head. "We will find it out but let's clear this mess first," Krishna responded, taking charge.

Three of them then quickly kept the agreements and the dresses from where it was all taken and ensured everything was in the same place before Rajamma arrived from work. Because as per Rajamma, Krishna doesn't know anything about the debts.

To Rajamma's surprise, the next morning Krishna got up early with roosters. With a strong willpower in his eyes, he took his bicycle and a clay *undiyal* (coin bank) with him and pedalled to the neighbouring town carefully ensuring the rattling *undiyal* in the basket didn't break.

• • •

As Krishna's village was located in a remote and arid area, all the women including Krishna's mother used to walk several kilometres to purchase vegetables and fruits, which they would then store for a week. Since he had accompanied his mother to the town a few times earlier, he knew the challenges faced by these women but he just chose to ignore them before. On the flip side, he had also witnessed agents unloading large rice bags at Kasi's shop while scratching lottery cards.

Suddenly Krishna hatched a plan: Why not supply fresh vegetables directly to the women in the village? Bridging the gap looked like a perfect solution to him—easing the women's burden and kickstarting his own venture.

However, that morning, when he approached an agent in the town market to help him sell fruits and vegetables in his village, the agent mocked and humiliated Krishna since he was so young. "Go, play with your toys kid," he sneered at Krishna. Without losing hope Krishna approached another agent but the insults only grew harsher—"You're too small for such big plans." Yet, Krishna didn't give up.

Fuelled by their insults, he bought a small selection of vegetables and greens with his *undiyal* money enough to begin his venture by selling to nearly eight to ten people in his village.

Upon reaching his village, Krishna unloaded his bicycle and arranged the vegetables on a rope cot, a *kattil*, in front of his house and commenced selling. Initially, villagers looked at Krishna's makeshift shop with puzzled smiles, as if it was a child's playset. However, after inquiring about the prices, one by one, they started buying from Krishna. Because he didn't add any profit for himself as he was clear with his strategy: attract customers first. That clever move remained a powerful seed for his bright future. Little did he know that his simple act was the beginning of something bigger.

After selling all the vegetables, again the next morning he cycled back to town to procure a fresh batch of vegetables with the money that he got from the previous day. He then came back to the village and restocked his *Kattil Kadai*.

This daily ritual of buying and selling eventually became his routine, a routine where profit was not the goal but merely the rotation of his *undiyal* funds. Though the to and fro was tiring, as per Krishna it was an effective business model that kept his entrepreneurial dreams alive and spinning.

However, Krishna was still a young boy, and it pained Rajamma to see him suffer working hard. Yet, she held back her emotions to make him understand the harsh realities of life.

I still clearly remember the day when I first met Krishna *Anna*, a thin boy in trousers. It was twenty-five years ago. His *Kattil Kadai* was near to my aunt's house. She sent me to buy half a kg of green brinjal from him while she was busy cooking.

Soon after my purchase, Krishna Anna noticed that I was just a young girl and kindly asked Ram Anna to make sure I got back to my aunt's house safely. Ram Anna agreed with a smile and took it upon himself to walk me home, chatting with me along the way to keep me at ease.

"You know what, Manju Aunty? Ram Anna held my hand till I came inside our compound," after coming home I told my aunty about the boys' kindness. She smiled nodding in agreement and remarked, "Krishna has been a blessing for the women in the village; now we don't have to walk a long distance for vegetables."

• • •

Over a period of time, Krishna's *Kattil Kadai* became well-known not just in his own village but also in the neighbouring ones, leading to increased demand. Now Krishna has to raise the supply to satisfy all. So, for the first time, he decided to keep a small profit which helped him buy more vegetables. The best part was, that despite the price adjustments, the villagers remained loyal customers because Krishna's prices were still reasonable. As a result, he soon increased the number of *Kattil* in front of his house.

Everything was going well, and Krishna began earning good money from his *Kattil Kadai*. However, his class teacher, who was also his customer, wasn't pleased to see him as a school dropout. Taking the initiative, she spoke to the school headmaster and managed to have him resume his education.

Even after returning to school, Krishna never gave up his *Kattil Kadai* as he was committed to repaying his father's debts. His days were long, he used to sell vegetables early in the morning and continued late into the night after school.

The good news was, after a lengthy absence, Kamala returned to the village. She was extremely happy and proud to hear about the transformation in Krishna and the boys. Yet, she was quite upset when she learned about the conflict between Krishna and his mother. It was Kamala who requested Rajamma to speak with Krishna once again.

Rajamma was content to see Kamala back but she had complaints. "Kamala, Why did you leave these boys? You were a guardian angel for them," Rajamma asked, her words heavy with emotion. Kamala couldn't say a lot as she also missed being around them. She knew how terrible it could have been for Rajamma to handle things alone. Kamala hugged Rajamma affectionately and said, "I will not go anywhere here afterwards, *Ma*."

• • •

Years passed.

Krishna performed well in his school and secured a seat in a nearby college. But by this time, he became the first person to establish a dedicated and big shop for fresh vegetables and fruits named "Rajamma Fruits & Vegetable Shop" in the village. Those agents who once insulted and underestimated Krishna were now supplying vegetables directly to his shop.

Krishna also helped the corn farmers in his village, and nearby areas by allowing them to use his shop as a platform to sell their harvest directly to customers at standard retail rates, without any commission for him. This selfless act not only aided the farmers to get fair prices but also brought the community closer together.

Finally, Krishna's relentless efforts bore fruit as he settled his father's debts, with interest. Ultimately his shop now became a landmark to the entire village.

"We knew years back that Krishna would become a big businessman," said the same villagers, who had once dismissed Krishna and his friends. Also, they admitted that "Rajamma is lucky to have Krishna as her son."

What else does a mother require from a son?

• • •

Krishna Anna might have made mistakes in the past without realising his mother's hard work but he had the maturity to make the right decision at the right time, that too at such a tender age.

Starting boldly with a small *Kattil Kadai* to a grand shop—Krishna Anna's story was inspirational not only to the people in his village but also to a small girl like me who visited the village only as a guest.

"Every success, big or small, comes with its own struggles and every achiever has a backstory that inspires," I remind myself at times when I end up doubting my journey.

Kamala moved to town after her wedding but her heart always stayed in the village. She used to come quite often to meet her squad. Hence, Krishna, Kamala, Ram and Lakshman remained as close friends as ever.

Life has its own way of bringing
people to us…

5

I Count Myself Lucky

"*Pillai nila irandum vellai nila...*" was a beautiful melody that she used to sing every single morning. In fact, singing was Deivaathal's unique way of making her workplace enjoyable. Starting from the time she stepped into the restroom with the cleaning supplies in hand, she would begin singing this particular song without fail. Then as she went about her everyday tasks—washing the sink, mopping the floor, and cleaning toilets, she would keep on switching songs. Sometimes, "*Malarnthum Malaratha...*" and sometimes "*Kadavul Ennum Muthalali...*".

Those days, my office routine often began with greeting Deivaathal, "Good Morning, *Ma*," because I used to go straight to the restroom soon after stepping in; to fix my hair, dress, and a little bit of touch-up. But deep inside my heart, I have always wanted to start my day by meeting Deivaathal first. Since I knew almost all the songs she sang, I used to start the first stanza while combing my hair, and she would then pick up where I left off. Further, she used to continue the harmonious loop while cleaning the big mirror and it was like a stress buster and one of the best things to kick off the day.

Honestly, even though those moments were short they were incredibly enjoyable and heartwarming. Eventually, I'd walk to my workplace humming a song and feeling fresh.

Knowingly or unknowingly Deivaathal was the one who taught me to find happiness in the simplest moments of our everyday work and a positive way to begin a day.

• • •

Deivaathal was the only one responsible for cleaning all the restrooms in our office. Think of how hectic it would be to clean the restrooms which were used by more than three hundred employees in a day, each visiting thrice at least. Yet, they always remained spotless and fresh, creating a pleasant experience for everyone who used them. On rainy mornings, our dirty shoes would sometimes spoil the freshly mopped white floors and we used to feel sorry for that but Deivaathal never showed any annoyance, instead, she would simply clean the mess again, all the while humming a cheerful tune.

From the neatly folded paper towels to the perfectly placed soap dispensers, apart from reflecting her dedication, everything spoke a lot about her care for every employee working there. "What would happen if Deivaathal took a day off...???" I would often ask my colleague, Dhanya after seeing Deivaathal's dedication and our dependence on her. But to our surprise, Deivaathal never took a single day's leave even when she was in need, knowing the worst condition of the restrooms would be. Moreover, she would also come on public holidays, voluntarily, to give a deep cleaning which was often not possible during regular days.

But this doesn't mean that Deivaathal was always in a happy mood or that her life was filled with sunshine and rainbows. She also had her own battles to fight with before coming to office every day.

One day, Dhanya and I had a chance to chat with Deivaathal in the restroom. Though it was a quick talk and her words were simple, it seemed like she opened up a book and flipped through stories about the tough times she faced in her life.

Deivaathal began her story by explaining how hard it was to find a job when she was suddenly tasked with raising her granddaughter all alone. At that point, she seemed to be desperately looking for a job to take care of the child. "Those times, I didn't even have enough money to afford bus fare. So I used to sell old vessels to manage job search and our expenditures," said Deivaathal with a lump in her throat.

To be frank, only after listening to Deivaathal's difficulty in finding a job, Dhanya and I realised how smoothly we both landed in our jobs.

Anyhow, Deivaathal's lack of literacy limited her job options at that time. She couldn't find the one she wanted and at last, ended up joining as a restroom cleaner in our office a decade ago. "So, this isn't the job you aspired to right? Then why do you put so much dedication into it when you could just do what you're paid for," we asked her, curious to know about her tireless commitment to a job which she hadn't sought.

"Whether I liked it or not, I was willing to take this job since I had a little girl at home who relied on me. Back then, this cleaning job was what helped me to put food on our table. So, how come I could take the job for granted? I will be forever grateful for it." Deivaathal's sincere response impacted us and honestly, it induced a sense of guilt within myself and Dhanya.

Deivaathal then continued sharing a bit about her other personal struggles as well—difficulties that nobody should endure. But the thing that I admired about her was, even with all that difficulty, Deivaathal never let her personal life affect her professional commitments and I never saw her coming up with silly excuses like my teammate, Shree, sitting in a fancy cubicle saying, "I do have personal problems at home, Sara, that's why I couldn't focus on my job," or Shilpa, "My husband is always fighting with me".

Deivaathal was a true professional and she made a long-lasting remark in my mind on that day. After hearing her, I also tried not to complain about work and ignored it when my colleagues did.

. . .

Unfortunately, there came a point when I had to part ways with that company. On my last day at work, I approached Deivaathal with a heart full of respect and affection. Because she was not just a professional inspiration for me, but a personal one as well. Whenever I was deeply worried I used to run to her to seek comfort and wisdom. Even though the interactions were not more than a few exchanged words or a shared smile, they were always impactful and offered relief. So I wanted to give her something as a gesture of my love towards her.

I said, "Ma, I'm leaving today. I'd like to give you something for all the love you have showered upon me. What would you like?"

However, on that day, when I asked her what she wanted, I had a couple of options in my mind that she would ask for, "a saree or a home appliance," but Deivaathal surprised me with her humble reply. The one that left me stunned and a little embarrassed.

"Madam, I couldn't ask for more in this life when I have everything I need. I consider myself blessed to be surrounded by kind-hearted people here who treat me as their own mother. This restroom is my little world of happiness, and I serve it with all my heart for others. I truly don't desire anything beyond this, please don't take me wrong."

"What a woman! And how beautifully said?" Deivaathal's heartfelt words made me speechless and it was a jarring moment of self-realisation that made me feel woefully inadequate and shallow. Here was a woman who found joy and purpose in serving others, while I had approached her with my own material expectations.

I then decided not to insist on further.

Living in a society where restroom cleaning was looked down upon and its workers were treated differently, Deivaathal stood tall, took extreme pride in her work, and considered it sacred. Only after speaking to her did I realise that I was supposed to be a humble taker from her forever rather than a giver. In fact, I had nothing to give her, instead, she had everything to give me. So that day, I bowed to her with respect and touched her feet to get her blessings, "Live long, madam!" Deivaathal wished me wholeheartedly and I left the office with a sense of fulfilment of being with a wonderful human so far.

• • •

As planned, within a few weeks, I found myself working in a new company. There and throughout my professional journey, I was frequently recognised for my dedication and my ability to maintain a cool headspace, regardless of work stress or personal problems.

"I'm just trying to do a little of Deivaathal," I would often tell my superiors in response to such honour and also acknowledging my respect for Deivaathal's work ethics. And each time I said that I counted myself lucky to have crossed paths with someone like her.

$$\mathbf{I}\text{t was a conscious decision}\ldots$$

6

Over to You

Every week, I used to visit a small library in a public park which was in a location called Ram Nagar. It was one such day, I went to the park to return the books that I had borrowed the previous week. As I stepped in at the other side of the park, I noticed Govind, the gardener and his wife Lakshmi engaged in a serious conversation with a woman and a little boy holding her hand, in a school uniform.

I never saw the woman or the kid earlier in the park. However, Govind, whom I knew well, spotted me from a distance and waved his hands, gesturing me to join their conversation.

When I went closer, the woman was requesting Govind to allow her plant a dozen saplings in the park. All seemed like native medicinal plants but the park was already overflowing with plants and trees; adding more may make it appear cluttered in the future. However, the woman insisted and went ahead to explain in detail, "I'm Indra, and this is my son, Ved. This year, his school took an inspiring initiative to distribute plants to all students at the end of the annual sports day celebration. I was so happy to see Ved receiving a neem sapling from his teacher but most parents were dissatisfied—calling it a cheap gift."

"What…???" Govind expressed his distress.

"Yeahh! They didn't value the sapling at all. Further, the parents came off with petty excuses like, 'We both are working and we don't have time to water plants' or 'We don't have enough space at home' and so on."

The small boy Ved also looked equally upset as she continued talking about how carelessly those parents treated the little saplings; they left them abandoned under the chairs and near the trash bins outside.

Indra and Ved then collected all the saplings in a jute bag and planted as much as possible in front and back of their house. When she still had many remaining, she went door to door in her neighbourhood with her son, asking for permission to plant them. Unfortunately, most of her neighbours turned down her request, stating that the roots could potentially harm their buildings in the future. But Indra did not argue with them as she knew it was pointless.

At last, when Indra had no other choice, she came to the park to plant all the remaining saplings.

I knew Govind very well; he wouldn't let those saplings die after hearing the backstory.

• • •

Actually, the park which we were seeing now—cool, breezy, and colourful—was not the same a few years ago. Though the park was in a renowned residential neighbourhood, it was pathetic and poorly maintained when it was handed over to Govind. It looked more like a haunted place with dry plants longing for water, half-dead trees, shrubs, and thorns everywhere. It also had inadequate lighting, damaged footpaths, and nasty restrooms. As a result, people who lived in the area never came to the park for walking or jogging.

Govind deserves every bit of praise. Even though he was a physically challenged person, driven by a deep desire to reconnect society with nature, he dedicated countless months, single-handedly, to transform the park.

He carefully selected each plant and nurtured them like his own children. He spent early mornings and late evenings tending to them, ensuring they received the right amount of water, sunlight, and care. Everyone knew Govind's devotion was not just about creating a beautiful space but about fostering a sanctuary where others could find peace and joy. And that was not at all an easy task—overcoming his challenges and meticulously pruning, planting, and nurturing every inch of the park's flora.

At last, his efforts paid off—the park gradually became popular among the locals. Govind's selflessness and passion turned a neglected area into a vibrant oasis.

The blooming flowers in the middle of the garden, the healthy trees, and the clean restrooms attracted nature lovers to come to the park regularly. He also made a kid's play area in one corner of the park with a merry-go-round and swings encouraging parents to bring their children to the park.

Over the time, Govind got married. Soon after their marriage, they were given a small space to live inside the park, which was not bigger than a typical motor room in India. They only had a small table fan, *korai pai* (grass mat), a few cooking items and at most ten dresses for each. But apart from materialistic scarcity, they had a great life.

Lakshmi was a kind-hearted woman and the right match for him, always helping him maintain the park and improve it. Now the park became even more beautiful with the combined efforts of Govind and his wife.

So I knew for sure that the kind-hearted couple, Govind and Lakshmi would help Indra and her son plant all the saplings.

"Why not? We will plant them in the park and take care of them daily. Don't worry," Govind assured Indra. "Thank you so much, *Anna*. But I don't want to trouble you, please help us with tools," Indra said.

"Oh! Sure," Govind rushed inside his room and brought the necessary tools to Indra. After explaining the procedure, he went to water the Jasmine plants nearby, leaving Lakshmi to assist Indra.

Indra was visibly relieved and she picked up a perfect spot near the big mango tree with the guidance of Lakshmi. But to my surprise, Indra didn't plant all those saplings herself, instead, she encouraged Ved to do it. She just stood nearby guiding and telling him stories about how she used to help her father with planting when she was a small girl to motivate Ved. Standing next to Indra, I was quietly watching the goodwill of those little hands and how happy he was while planting the saplings.

"Listen to me Ved, these twelve saplings have lives. Treat them as your siblings; you are the one responsible for watering them daily before you go to school, not the Gardener Uncle. You got it, *kannu*…???" she said cupping his cute little face and dusting his uniform after he finished planting everything. Ved, in turn, seemed thrilled to hear that he could come to the park daily. Thus he responded with a thumbs-up and cheerful nod, "*Hmm… Sari Amma*".

Indra then hugged Ved tightly, asked him to say "thank you" to Lakshmi and headed towards the play area, waving me goodbye.

"*Akka*, Indra doesn't look like a regular mother, no?" I remarked after observing them.

"True. She's something different," responded Lakshmi Akka, while both of us admiringly watched Indra and Ved enter the play area. With that exchange, Lakshmi Akka returned to her work, and I made my way to the library.

• • •

I recorded the date and time in the register and returned the books to their designated shelves. Govind was the one who diligently managed the library as well. Due to his physical challenges, people who came to the library never failed to put the books back on the appropriate shelves. We knew it would be difficult for him to rearrange the books if they were misplaced, especially those on the top shelves.

After returning the books, I had some time so I thought of taking a stroll in the park; it was indeed a bliss to be amidst the scent of flowers.

Simply, I was lost in my thoughts and every step I took was filled with gratitude to nature. However, I was also continually distracted by the sight of the three-year-old girl child, Thendral, on each round I took. She seemed to be feeling lonesome, watching all the kids playing and having fun together.

Thendral then approached a group of boys and girls playing nearby and asked if she could join them. But sadly, they refused her request. It was indeed distressing to see the child's disappointment, but I didn't take it too seriously, knowing that such incidents are quite common among children. "They'll be okay when I come back for the next round," I told myself.

As expected, after some time, the group of kids agreed to play with Thendral. She was the youngest, so they kept her in the middle of the circle and danced to the nursery rhyme "Ring

A Ring O' Roses". Though the little one couldn't comprehend the lyrics, she kept on clapping whenever they said, "A-tishoo! A-tishoo! We all fall down!"

Seeing them playing together and innocently giggling, I found myself teleported to the days of my childhood, singing the same rhyme with my friends. Further, when I looked around, the parents of these kids were also gathered behind, watching them play with Thendral. Considering the parents' ages, I thought they too would be reminiscing about their carefree childhood like me. But I also happened to notice a stark contrast—though most faces were aglow with nostalgia, to my surprise, others wore expressions of discomfort and disdain.

Thendral's dark skin, messy hair, and pitiful look didn't allow them to accept the fact that their kids were playing with her. And above all, there was a lady who constantly kept pushing Thendral out of the circle. Unaware of why she was being pushed away or realising that she was being mistreated, poor Thendral, went on re-entering the circle repeatedly and kept clapping and jumping, continuing the game innocently.

The lady's frustration grew with each unsuccessful attempt to push Thendral away. Over time, her patience snapped, and she harshly dragged the little girl out of the circle, hurling hurtful words at her. Thendral's little eyes widened with confusion and pain.

Tears streamed down her cheeks as she hit the ground.

It was heart-wrenching to see the sight of her tiny body trembling and her knees scraped and bleeding. But the lady, devoid of any compassion, coldly turned her back and walked away, leaving Thendral sobbing on the ground.

"Is she a human?" I gasped. My heart ached for the poor girl who did nothing to deserve this harsh treatment but before I could reach Thendral to offer help, she rushed in like a heroine to rescue the girl—The young mother, Indra.

Indra quickly took Thendral near the first aid box and gave her a treatment to prevent aggravation of the injury. The pain was so intense for Thendral that she continued to cry, pointing at her scratches for quite some time. Despite Indra's attempt to console her, Thendral didn't stop weeping. So, Indra took her to the restroom, requesting me to watch over her son, Ved. I agreed and assumed that she was going inside to comfort Thendral.

However, twenty minutes passed, and they did not come out. Concerned about Thendral, I entered the restroom to see what was happening.

When I stepped in, I didn't hear the child crying anymore; her hair was no longer messy, and she didn't look pitiful. The moment I caught a glimpse of her reflection in a tiny mirror, it was a sight I would never forget. Thendral's eyes sparkled as she admired herself in the mirror, a shy smile spreading across her face. She turned this way and that, marvelling at her transformation, her little fingers gently touching her clean, combed hair.

Altogether, she looked like a little angel in her yellow shirt and blue trousers, her appearance glittering with innocence and joy.

Since Thendral's skirt tore out when she was dragged, Indra was generous enough to give her a bath, brush her hair, and dress her in Ved's birthday dress which she bought while coming to the park. Indra had not only cleaned and dressed up Thendral but had also restored her dignity and joy.

I'm sure Indra wasn't economically richer than the lady who dragged Thendral. But Indra showed what she was more rich at—humanity. Thendral's transformation was more than just a change of clothes; it was a demonstration of Indra's compassion.

Even though I was truly moved to see her empathy, it in turn made me question my actions—Why hadn't I done more to Thendral as Indra did? I would have merely helped with the first aid, not considering anything beyond that. In fact, none of us in the crowd had this thought. Indra, indeed, had a big heart and a broad mind to give her son's dress which he had to wear the next day.

As soon as it struck me that I did nothing for Thendral, I hurriedly took her to the lady who dragged her out.

"Do you even know who she is? Her father has dedicated his life to creating this green paradise for all of us, including your son. You mark my words, a few years later, your son will not appreciate what you have done today, but he will remember Govind forever." Further, I warned the lady never to ill-treat any kids again and walked away with Thendral.

The lady became deathly silent after hearing me, but I don't think she realised what she did was wrong. "Anyway, she is setting a bad example for her son," I consoled myself.

"Oh, is she the gardener's daughter?" one of the parents next to her asked while I came back. "It seems to be," the other one confirmed.

Once I returned to Indra, she asked Ved to take Thendral to the play area and urged him to hold onto the child tightly while they swung. In fact, in the care of Indra and Ved, Thendral seemed to forget what had happened to her and she became happy.

They soared back and forth on the swing. It was so overwhelming to see the children, their faces lit up with pure delight—their laughter filled the air, pure and untainted by any notion of discrimination.

It was very clear that children like Ved and Thendral saw each other as only playmates, free from the societal divisions of wealth, gender, or class. It also reflected Indra's remarkable character as she fostered such profound values, a sense of equality and compassion in her son. Unlike other parents, Indra found genuine happiness in seeing the children play together and hearing their shared laughter. Her eyes welled up with tears, witnessing their unblemished joy.

For me, Indra's actions spoke louder than words, showcasing her as a rare and beautiful soul who understood the true essence of raising children to be kind and empathetic individuals.

• • •

That garden scene is still fresh in my mind.

Whenever I see little children playing around, I remember Indra—the young, kind, and visionary mother, and I often end up saying, "She is a different mother."

That day, I had a word with Indra when Ved and Thendral were playing together. I told her the same words, "You are a different mother!". But she just laughed it off as if she didn't do anything bigger. Yet, after the conversation took shape, I slowly understood why this was such an ordinary thing for her.

"It's a conscious decision that my husband and I made when we were pregnant with Ved. We didn't want to take the pregnancy for granted from day one. Instead, we saw it as our duty to raise our child to be a responsible citizen." Indra told it genuinely from her heart and I could sense the responsibility and pride while she said that.

She further continued, "My husband was the one who instilled this clarity in me. When we were pregnant, he often said, 'If you wish to do something good for the nation, raise your children to be good.'

Also, he strongly believed that only young parents hold a potential tool—their children—who can make significant social change in the future.

So, we both embraced it as our duty and to be honest, we are also becoming better humans along with Ved now." Indra's response left me amazed, because, in my experience, when someone finds out they're pregnant, the first thing they do is make a grand announcement of the news to their loved ones followed by a series of celebrations over the next few months. And once the baby arrives, they hope their child can accomplish all that they couldn't; starting from their career choices to owning a luxury car.

But when I was listening to Indra's words I was wondering how many parents would consider pregnancy as their duty to raise their child as a responsible citizen of the country. Indra and her husband were deliberate in every action they took and I was in awe of them.

On that day, though I was unmarried, she invoked a future mother lying somewhere inside me urging me to recognise the gravity of parenthood.

"Upbringing a child is not a casual job. It's a responsibility."—Indra told me with a sisterly concern.

Well, setting an example for me, Indra left the park. Now, it's over to every young parent to make a conscious decision…

That's how she met him…

7
Decided Forever

"So, where did you go recently? Did you try the local food there…?" This was her all-time favourite question whenever we had our get-togethers. Janu, my dear friend and a big foodie, loved non-vegetarian dishes. Whenever we met she would eagerly ask about every dish we had since our last meeting and then jot it down on her "to-taste" list, hoping to eat them someday.

One evening, Poorni, Vijay, Janu, and I, gathered at my house. "So… where did you all go recently?" As usual, Janu initiated the topic with her signature question. Since the four of us were meeting after a long time, she wanted to know every single detail of our travel shenanigans to update her list and find a new experience to try.

Vijay started and talked about the mouth-watering roadside delicacies he enjoyed on a business trip to Delhi, like spicy *chole bhature* and crispy *jalebis*. Poorni shared her experience at a new restaurant, raving about the flavourful *biryani* and rich *mutton curry* she had there. I excitedly recounted my unplanned journey through the "City of Thousand Temples"— Kanchipuram, and a quaint village nearby, enjoying the unique flavours at every stop.

Janu then recollected her trip to Kerala, exclaiming, "Oh, guys, you know? The seafood in Kerala was a revelation! I never tasted anything like that before. The tenderness of the fish and the richness of the crabs were simply unparalleled." Honestly, Janu's energy and involvement in the narration almost transported us straight to the sea. She described the mouth-watering grilled fish marinated with coastal spices, the crab curry with a rich, tangy tomato base, and the prawns cooked in a fragrant coconut milk sauce. We could almost taste the spicy fish fry and the buttery lobster, dripping with herbs and garlic through her words.

Soon after hearing about her intriguing seafood stories, we were eager to plan a similar trip for the upcoming holiday. However, we needed to find a new destination since Janu didn't want to repeat her Kerala adventure.

So, every one of us came up with a new destination, but it quickly gave way to a flurry of conflicting opinions and playful rebuttals.

"How about Goa?" Poorni suggested.

"In this heat? We'll melt on the beach," Vijay countered.

"Then what about Puri?" I chimed in.

"Too far," Janu shook her head. "We'd spend half our vacation just getting there and back."

"Hogenakkal? We could eat fresh fish there," Vijay tried again.

"It'll be packed with tourists this time of year," Poorni sighed.

"Pondicherry?" Janu offered hopefully.

"No no…Been there twice already," I said to her.

Finally, it was Vijay who broke the cycle. After seeing a glimpse of a travel vlog on his phone featuring a family catching live fish and cooking them with Indian flavours, he exclaimed, "This is the place and it's not so far. Let's catch and cook!" His excitement was contagious; he wanted us to watch the vlog together to convince us.

Since none of us had ever gone fishing, we were curious to see what was in the video that made Vijay so excited. We quickly arranged a cosy movie night set up and settled in to watch the lengthy vlog with our anticipation buzzing in the air.

• • •

The video began rolling from the vlogger's house, outlining their day's plan and showcasing all the homemade snacks and drinks they packed for the trip.

Like Vijay said, it was a family trip of a content creator couple—Rupa and Murali. Rupa gave a quick introduction of how Murali and her children—Isha and Dev, were preparing for the trip, and had started to load the necessary stuff in the car for the day.

Rupa and Murali were not only creators, but they seemed to be explorers and this time they had set off to explore a lake in the outskirts of the city, famous for fishing.

As they drove, Rupa captured every bit of the scenery for their followers. The trip seemed to be nice and smooth but unexpectedly, the path turned bumpy and deserted within an hour. Rupa started worrying and voiced her concern when Murali took a couple of wrong turns, "Murali, this route is trickier than we thought," she said with a hint of fear in her voice about being late to the fishing spot. Yet, as time went by, the beauty of the journey kept her vlogging, and she continued narrating every scene she saw.

Finally, they arrived at the fishing spot after an exhilarating five-hour journey.

"Though it took a little longer to reach, this place is totally worth it," said Murali, attracted by gentle waves. "Exactly! It's wonderful. Let's make the most of every minute," said Rupa panning the camera towards the kids; her tiredness overshadowed her enthusiasm.

Rupa quickly started setting up the rod for fishing. Murali played a dual role, assisting Rupa with the rod while also filming the video for her.

When we saw all those things, the video looked so captivating that we all wished to be instantly teleported to that picturesque spot. The children, though new to fishing, radiated joy as they watched their parents and absorbed every detail of the process. Their enthusiasm was infectious, and soon we found ourselves on the edge of our seats, hearts racing with excitement as we imagined our future fishing expedition. The prospect of such an adventure had us practically leaping off the sofa in enthusiasm.

But disappointingly, Rupa's first few attempts captured only smaller fish, which she released back into the water. "Look at her patience!" Poorni exclaimed, impressed by Rupa's determination.

However, as time went by, despite her repeated attempts at catching and dropping, she neither caught big fish nor could she bear the sun. Eventually, like a small girl, Rupa became cranky and wanted to give up but Murali lightened up her mood with his witty jokes and encouraged her to try one more time. "This is the real essence of fishing," Vijay said.

Even though Rupa failed every time, their engaging interactions, filled with laughter and mutual support, kept us glued to the screen.

We gradually started rooting for Rupa as if we were present there with her. We felt every near-miss and celebrated each small victory.

Subsequently, Rupa seemed to learn the tricks of the trade and caught medium-sized fish one after another. "She did it at last!" Janu cheered more than any of us and was visibly thrilled whenever Rupa got sizable catches.

"Hmm…Fishing seems to be adventurous, right? Why don't we give it a shot somewhere nearby this weekend?" Vijay proposed energetically and didn't want to wait for a holiday to go fishing. "Sounds like a plan," I replied, matching his enthusiasm. "Oh God! Will someone let me watch the videooo!!!" Poorni annoyingly said, resuming the video.

By this time, the video neared its end, and Rupa had caught enough fish. "Murali, I'm going to drop all of them into the icebox, you look for a shaded area," saying that Rupa went near to their car to drop all the fish in the icebox. In the meantime, as Rupa instructed, Murali was looking for a cool, shaded spot where they could enjoy the snacks they had brought along.

One after another, Rupa transferred the fishes into the icebox, their silvery scales glinting in the sunlight. Yet she kept the last one aside to demonstrate to her viewers how to remove the hook from its mouth. "Look at my hand guys," Rupa said to her viewers, bringing the last fish closer to the camera, "Now, I'm going to show you all how to remove this hook." The fish wriggled in her grasp as she positioned it for a clear view.

"It's essential to learn," Poorni acknowledged Rupa's intention. Little did we know that this seemingly educational moment was about to trigger a profound emotion in one of us.

What we witnessed in the next clip was far from educational—it was a brutal awakening that left us all shaken to our core.

Saying 1, 2 and 3, Rupa yanked the hook out of its tiny mouth without any care, as if the fish didn't feel anything. Even though the fish wasn't making a sound, we could almost hear its cries of pain in our heads. "Rupa, that's awful! You can't do that!" shouted Janu.

What made it even worse was watching Isha and Dev, the vlogger's young children. They were laughing and giggling as the fish struggled. These kids were so young and innocent that they didn't understand what was really happening. They couldn't see that the fish was suffering—to them, it probably looked like a funny dance or a game.

We knew that the kids weren't being mean on purpose but their laughter, usually a happy sound, felt wrong and upsetting in that situation. "Look at the video, it's that easy to trick kids to make them believe that hurting animals is okay," Janu was in shock. "They are so naive," Poorni added.

"The scene is like a wake-up call, isn't it? These little kids will believe everything we adults do," we looked at each other thinking about how our simple actions affect children.

As we continued our conversation and discussed how disappointing the video was, we saw that the wounded fish tried to escape from Rupa's hand and fell to the ground but the poor fish was not lucky. Isha picked it up from the floor and dropped it into the icebox, closing the lid with a loud thud.

"*Pothum*, it's enough watching," we all said in unison as the video became too much to bear. Vijay stopped playing it immediately. On the other hand, the unsettling clips made us reconsider our fishing plans as well. Everyone looked a little sad and no one felt like talking to each other. Poorni and Vijay got up to leave for their home. Meanwhile, Janu went to the balcony, seemingly lost in her thoughts.

"Hey wait, guys! She seemed to be disturbed," I shared a glance with Vijay and Poorni.

"Don't worry. Give her some time, she'll be fine," Poorni reassured me. With that Vijay and Poorni waved goodbye and left my house.

"What happened Janu? What's wrong?" I went to the balcony to speak with her.

"How could I have been so blind all these years, Sara?" Janu said with regret.

"You know me very well, fish is my favourite seafood, especially fried fish. I've had it at least half a million times throughout my life. But I never realised that I was enjoying the taste of a frightened fish."

"Janu, don't take the video personally. Do you wanna watch some feel-good movies? Let's watch something, come," I tried taking her focus off the video.

"No Sara, you are not getting it. After watching the video, I can't even imagine how suffocating those last moments would have been for all those fish in that small ice-box," Janu expressed in her guilt-struck voice. "And the kids laughing? It feels like we're teaching them something wrong."

Hearing Janu's words, I was moved. Until then I hadn't truly realised the weight of the video on Janu. I couldn't stand by; I went close to her and offered comfort, "Playing that video was a mistake," I told myself. Further, the seriousness on her face made me a little hesitant to talk to her.

Anyhow, while I was trying my best to convince her, Janu suddenly came up with a shocking decision that she wanted to give up non-vegetarian food for the rest of her life.

"What??? Listen! It's a big decision and quite the commitment, Janu," I raised my voice to give her a caution. "Think twice. For someone like you, who is fond of non-veg food, it will be a difficult decision in the long run," I wanted her to give it a second thought.

But Janu wasn't ready to reconsider her decision. "No, I don't want to reconsider. You're just thinking about me, Sara, but fish also have lives. In fact all animals do, right?" Janu countered me strongly. "It seems the clip impacted you so deeply but I have a feeling that this sudden resolve will not stand longer," I attempted once more to reason with her, yet Janu remained immovable.

• • •

Time marched on, and with each passing week, Janu proved me wrong. Her resolve, which I had once doubted, was enduring—it seemed her decision was not a fleeting impulse but a steadfast dedication.

One day when I expressed my admiration for her commitment and asked her the secret to sticking to her decision, Janu said, "Because I'm very clear about why I took the decision."

Janu was actually right, when she was certain about the reasons, the transition was neither hard nor did she crave non-vegetarian food. Yet her only concern was her family. She didn't reveal the decision to them as she was afraid they wouldn't accept it. And of course, they didn't.

They were greatly worried and tried to convince her that she would become weak if she suddenly gave up non-veg food. However, as time went by, and her parents saw her being healthy and stable, her mother proudly began to share Janu's decision with her friends and relatives. This acceptance and support from her family became a source of encouragement for Janu, reinforcing her decision even further.

The very moment when Janu's family embraced her decision, she became so happy and relieved that she was no longer required to answer anyone. But to Janu's dismay, the real challenge began after that. She was subjected to a multitude of dumb questions thrown at her by society. Most of her relatives were meat eaters, so they couldn't understand what Janu was going through when they made fun of her vow.

Though it was hurting Janu, she simply dusted it off and moved on, as she didn't want to tap on everybody's shoulder to explain, "Why did she quit non-veg?"

. . .

Janu was okay and ignored people for a couple of years but there came a stage in her life when she couldn't just sweep things under the rug and had to deal with the hurt—Janu's family started seeing an alliance for her.

There was no reason Janu's parents would want to hide her food habits, they clearly mentioned it in her matrimonial profile.

Seeing her profile, a few parents from the prospective groom's side would straightforwardly say no, mentioning that they were specifically seeking a non-vegetarian. Janu was fine with such honest responses from the very beginning. However, what she was not fine with were the incidents when the groom's family initially portrayed themselves as open-minded and modern, and once everything was fixed they would reveal their true expectations, insisting that she needed to change; aptly showcasing that the girl's decision wasn't a big deal for them.

It was shocking for Janu as she didn't expect that a simple thing like quitting non-veg food would cause this much trouble to her. Despite all of this, including society's ugly remarks and wedding rejections, Janu stood firm and didn't give it a second thought—not even once. She considered it a phase of life. During this time, one day, Janu's parents arranged a call with a prospective groom, Sanjay.

"I'm working in IT and I'm earning well there. I like cricket a lot. I hope you won't bother when I go to the ground on weekends after our marriage. Cricket is everything to me.

And Janu, I wanted to tell you something else also. Though I belonged to a vegetarian family, I switched to meat when I moved to Bangalore and my family doesn't know this," said Sanjay in a dictatorial voice, almost trying to say that Janu should not spill this news to his family. Though Sanjay seemed a bit rough, Janu liked his openness and she absolutely had no problem with his change in food habits.

But as she further listened to Sanjay, he was continuously talking about his likes, dislikes, and expectations in a relationship and his reluctance to cook or take care of household chores after marriage.

Similarly, Janu also had a lot to say to Sanjay, so she waited for her turn to speak. But the guy didn't even give a small gap for her to fill up, instead, he assumed that the conversation was all about him and his family.

In places like my hometown, parents don't usually allow much time for the prospective bride and groom to converse over the phone before marriage. So, when Janu realised that Sanjay wasn't going to give her a chance to speak, she interrupted.

"Sanjay, I understand that you switched to meat and you like it a lot now—I'm ok with that—but I hope you're fully aware of my eating habits which are contrary to yours..." Janu wanted to reassure him as it was her primary concern.

Janu was willing to make any adjustments in married life provided her vow wasn't disturbed by her partner and family.

"Yeah, your family told me and my parents about your eating habits earlier, but I'm confident you will change your mindset as time passes after marriage and that will prove your love for me, won't you?" As assumed, he gave a baseless response and left Janu wondering, "Does proving love necessitate sacrificing a vow?"

"Such a selfish guy, Sara. I don't know how he presumed that I would change," Janu was very upset when she told me about that whole disheartening incident later.

So, on that day, after listening to his nonsensical theories about love, Janu hung up the call with polite words.

However, the guy didn't stop there. Being an IT professional in a big firm earning handsome money, his ego got hurt by this rejection. As he got to know that his theories of love would not influence Janu, he immediately called her mother and started shouting rudely with his logic, "If your daughter treats all living beings equally then why is she still consuming vegetables every meal? And why is she even drinking milk which is secreted for calves? Or is she planning to improve the fishermen's economy when everyone stops eating fish???" His words clearly proved that firstly, he doesn't know how to respect anyone, and secondly, his partner's choices don't matter to him. Sanjay just flushed out his irritation on her mother.

"Now, along with me, my family is also pushed to answer these pointless questions, Sara. It's my personal choice and I never forced anyone to change their habits then why he spoke like that?" Janu became so emotional saying that. However, what I admired the most was that nothing broke her vow—She neither gave up, nor her family asked her to change her mind.

But after that incident, Janu became more rigid and self-sufficient. Eventually, she started hating the concept of marriage altogether. Still, her family quietly continued searching for the right match for her, hoping to find someone who would appreciate and respect her choices.

. . .

Finally, to my happiness, after a few years, Janu got to speak with the man of her life—Arjun.

"Is this your biggest worry?" Arjun burst out into laughter after hearing her concern. "It's your choice, and it's up to you," that's all he said. Following that, they both continued sharing their thoughts about relationship and marriage and it looked like an effortless exchange. They didn't specifically mention their desires, it automatically fitted in during the call.

And that's how Janu and Arjun got married.

After their wedding, and till today, they have taken several international trips where finding vegetarian food was quite challenging. Arjun would patiently hold her hand and take her to restaurant after restaurant until he found a suitable place for Janu.

Moreover, being a meat lover, Arjun never cooked or asked Janu to cook meat at home. Even though Janu was willing to cook for her dear husband, he was concerned that the smell of cooking meat might cause her discomfort. Therefore, he chose to have non-vegetarian food at restaurants.

I was thrilled that my dearest friend found a good partner, after what she has faced all these years. "You both are so lucky to have each other, Janu. All those struggles you went through have paid off at last. I am so happy seeing you guys together." I blessed them from the bottom of my heart once I visited their home.

The tale of Arjun and Janu is a strong reminder that one day we will find someone who cherishes us for exactly how we are;

not for what we eat, what we wear, how we look or what brand names we know; but will cherish us for our mere existence in their life, and this unconditional acceptance is called true love.

It's been many years now but Arjun hadn't changed his food habits for Janu and she didn't switch back for her husband. For them, food habit was such a small thing and what really mattered was mutual respect for each other's individuality.

It's decided on forever… !!!

Silence…

8

Why Don't I Cry?

As a small girl, I used to be very naughty, and I ended up getting punishments from my mother quite often—usually, ten sit-ups. But every time I was punished, instead of quietly accepting it, I'd immediately run straight to my *Periyamma* (Mother's elder sister) to complain. I was a drama queen those days—"See Periyamma, *Amma* is always rough with me! Do you think I would have broken that glassware???" I used to sob clutching Periyamma's saree and stage a sympathetic scene to make her believe my mother was a villainess and I was innocent.

Periyamma was a woman of pure motherliness. She didn't know anything beyond showing love and affection to others, especially to me. She saw only the best in me, no matter what I did was right or wrong and we both indeed shared a magical connection. So whenever I complained to her she would put aside all her work and walk me back to my mother, although she knew I was the troublemaker.

"Never again should you punish my sweet little angel," Periyamma used to roar, narrowing her eyes at my mother. Meanwhile, my mother who had immense respect for her sister kept herself quiet for punishing me. "Sorry Amma, I can't help you," I would sense all my drama and say this to myself, laughter bubbling up within me.

But when I think about it now, those were the funniest moments from my childhood that never fail to bring a smile to my face.

Periyamma was indeed my fortress and my biggest support, spoiling me with her love and affection. As I grew, I mostly stayed in her house which was just two streets away from mine. Despite having three daughters of her own, Sudha, Maha and Radha, I was often the recipient of her extra care and attention; be it in the form of chocolates, gifts, or kisses and hugs. Of course, this sometimes stirred a bit of jealousy in my cousins, but it was short-lived. We actually were a close-knit bunch, eating together, playing together, sleeping together, and of course doing mischief together!

However, when I finished my schooling, I had to relocate to pursue my higher education. By that time, more than leaving my mother, I was sad about leaving Periyamma. I vividly remember the first time I left my home for college, Periyamma handed me a glass jar full of cashews, almonds, and some money. She didn't say a lot but her eyes curiously asked me, "When will you come back, *kannu*?" That was the moment I understood that this separation was going to be tougher than I expected, for both me and Periyamma.

I could not reply to Periyamma that day, as I got numb seeing her emotionally weak. Thereafter, whenever I returned to my hometown, first I would rush to Periyamma's house and then I'd go home. We would then start counting down to my next holiday.

• • •

Graduation years passed like that and now I have become a working woman. Yet my love and affection for Periyamma never changed. In fact, I started realising that Periyamma was growing older too. As everyone knows Periyamma was a caring woman and she took care of everyone around her but she didn't pay attention to her health issues. So, every time I went to my hometown, along with the excitement of seeing her, there was also a deep itching fear while leaving. Fear of not getting a chance to see her the next time I am home.

One day while I was in a conference room presenting something important, I got an emergency call from my cousin Radha. "Amma is no more, Sara, come soon…" she managed to say but shiveringly. I couldn't believe my ears and my world shattered right there.

After the call, I was not even able to move a single slide of my presentation. Following that I got a call from my mother, echoing the same devastating news. Meanwhile, I cannot be thankful enough to my manager and colleagues. They were the ones who understood the intensity of the situation I was in and handled it well. They helped me to leave sooner saying, "Don't bother about this presentation, Sara. Just freeze everything, we will take care of it." With their help, I left the office soon.

I hurriedly caught a train whichever was available at "Chennai Central Railway Station" at that time and I rushed to my hometown.

Every minute on the train looked like an hour for me. I was hungry and tired, moreover, thoughts of Periyamma left me overwhelmed with grief. "Who would look after me as you?

How would I console my three cousins in the face of such a loss?" These painful questions were running back and forth in my mind until I arrived home.

Since my journey was a little longer than expected, by the time I arrived, my Periyamma had already been taken away. "How can you all do this to me???" I shouted in anger and frustration. Unwilling to accept the reality of not being able to see her face for one last time. I adamantly demanded to see Periyamma. But all I have seen there were nothing but guilt-stricken faces in front of me. Eventually, when I got no response from people there, I went inside Periyamma's house angrily.

I barely noticed the relatives, neighbours and others sitting in the living room. I was completely exhausted and could only focus on a big photo frame of Periyamma in the middle of the room, which was captured on her last birthday. I went straight to it and knelt down silently, beginning to grieve and pay my respects.

"Why were you in this hurry, Periyamma? You could have waited for me to come to see your face at least. What do I do now? Tell me!" My eyes became heavy now and I knew she was listening to me from the other side of the photo frame. When a beautiful bond was unfolding between me and my dear Periyamma, I was interrupted. "Amma was so adamant…" Sudha Akka, my eldest cousin, knelt down next to me and began with a choked voice.

"When Amma was in her last few minutes she compelled me to open the cupboard. Though there were a lot of sarees, she urged me to pull the brand-new blue saree from the top shelf. And she got a promise from me that the particular saree should be covered on her when she was taken to the burial ground. Amma loves you more than any of us, Sara." Sudha Akka's words echoed in the room and she hugged me tightly.

I got more emotional after hearing Sudha Akka. I vividly remember, the blue saree she was talking about was the first gift I bought for my Periyamma from my own earnings. The memory of her rejoiced face at receiving my gift that day was still fresh in my mind as I listened to Sudha Akka. However, I never knew that she kept the saree as a treasure and wanted to take it with her on her last journey. "I love you Periyamma," I said silently to her and closed my eyes one more time to resume my prayers.

"What kind of girl is she? Heartless! She didn't shed even a single drop of tear hearing Sudha," a lady commented on me.

"Yeah, looks so arrogant," the other one replied.

"This girl used to come quite often here," one of the neighbouring ladies raised her voice as if she wanted me to hear her. "Yes, Yes! Saraswathi treated the girl like her own daughter. This girl used to eat here, sleep here and exploit her Periyamma in the name of love. Look at her now, she is showing her real face." The ladies' comments were truly hurtful but despite hearing her, I didn't give back or want to. Instead, after lighting a small clay lamp to Periyamma, I quietly left the room.

I came out and sat under the *pantal*, a temporary shed, and tried to console my cousin Radha who was constantly weeping. When I looked around, there were a lot of men sitting under the pantal, including my Periyamma's husband. Though they were sad about the loss, none of them cried. In places like my hometown, it's often found unusual for men to cry even at condolences which reflects their mental fortitude.

But after seeing them, I was truly taken aback questioning why I was the only one being targeted by those ladies for not crying. Meanwhile, Sudha Akka rushed out to see me and said, "Don't take those ladies personally, Sara."

• • •

That day I didn't respond to Sudha Akka because that was not the first time I heard such hurtful comments. I'm used to it in every condolence and am often judged as a heartless and emotionless person. So I simply smiled back at Sudha Akka and headed to my home to take the ritual bath.

When I look back a few years, I still get shivers due to a devastating incident—my father's demise.

My father was a man of high moral standards and an exceptional human being. But 13 years ago, when I saw him lying silently before me, I felt like I was standing in the middle of a crossroads, having to face my challenges all alone. Because that was something I didn't see coming and it was obviously an unbearable loss for me.

On that day, after seeing my father in such a condition, my mind completely accepted that he wouldn't wake up but my heart was still longing for him to get up and talk to me. So I kept my father's head on my lap not wanting any of the relatives to come closer to him. "He didn't die. Don't put garlands on him…" I didn't even allow them to perform the custom they usually do for the deceased, insanely believing that my father would come back.

Also, I tried to wake him up a couple of times by gently tapping on his cheeks, "Wake up *Appa*," but he didn't respond. When I had no other option to get him back, I started crying uncontrollably and shouting loudly while holding his head. Because I was unable to express my love, fear, and insecurities in any other form.

However, I witnessed several people around me expressing their emotions in their own ways during that difficult time. Some cried for my father like me, some with lesser tears, some crocodile tears, and even a few happy tears intending to get property shares. Men mostly didn't cry. It was on that day that I came to realise grief is an intensely personal journey.

Soon after my father's death, I was inevitably exposed to the ugly side of life and had to learn to cope with things on my own and it was tougher than I expected. Many days, when I couldn't handle my challenges, I used to switch off all the lights in my room and I cried uncontrollably begging him to return. But he never returned as any of the departed ever did—only my eyes dried.

Thereafter, life automatically pushed me to the next phase to find strength within and to face challenges all alone.

I slowly picked myself up and started growing mentally. Further, I learnt to see life with new eyes and began understanding the deeper meaning behind life and death.

"Every soul comes with a unique purpose to Mother Earth and it departs once it's fulfilled. I too will depart when my purpose has been met." As soon as I realised this reality, I stopped asking for my father to come back and I stopped crying in condolences as well. Instead, I feel relaxed for the departed souls including my father's who would have gone to a better place after finishing their earthly duties.

So, paying silent grief is my way of dealing with emotions and I don't believe I owe anyone an explanation for "Why don't I cry?" in condolences.

Small minds…

9

A Woman with a Moustache

Sarita was 40 years old when I met her. Born and brought up in a remote village in the North-western part of Tamil Nadu, her childhood was simple like any other family in that village.

Her father worked tirelessly in the fields, her mother ran the household, and she, being the only child, was their everything. Sarita's parents were not wealthy but her needs were always met. She was raised with tender care and affection, more like in a fairy tale. When Sarita turned 18, her elderly parents began to worry about her future, constantly wondering who would take care of her after they were gone. So, when they learned about a suitable boy in a nearby town, they decided to get her married to him immediately.

Despite Sarita's reluctance to get married at such a young age, she never opposed it. She chose to marry the one her father had selected because she held his words in high regard.

Fortunately, her father's choice turned out to be a blessing. Kanna was not just a good husband but also a true gentleman and a man ahead of his time. Recognizing Sarita's passion for her studies he encouraged her to continue it even after their marriage. With Kanna's moral support, Sarita completed her B.A. in Tamil literature and, after taking a year's break, she went on to earn her Master's Degree as well.

Both Sarita and Kanna remained side by side with each other in every other aspect of life and the first nine years of their marriage were absolutely blissful. However, despite their wonderful life, they lacked something in their little world—a child. They couldn't conceive in these nine years. Though it didn't bother the couple because of the fulfilment they felt in each other's company, they were severely humiliated by their relatives at every gathering. Sarita was especially the one who often bore the brunt of their harsh words.

In the beginning, she managed to shrug off the comments with Kanna's moral support but she was deeply disturbed when Kanna's mother insinuated that Sarita was having some problems with her body. After all, in those days, the societal recognition of a woman's greatest achievement and the ultimate validation of a happy married life was having a baby.

As time went by, the expectation of having a child weighed heavily on Sarita, making her feel extremely inadequate as a woman—a pain that no one should go through. At one point, when Sarita found the hurtful comments increasingly difficult to bear, she decided to quit her beloved teaching job.

Further, in search of a solution, she started taking various treatments one after another from the ancient wisdom of Siddha and Ayurveda to the modern approaches of Allopathy. Yet, nothing helped them. Over the years, despite their persistent efforts, Sarita and Kanna couldn't find success. The poor couple grew tired day by day. Eventually, they decided to step back from the exhausting cycle of treatments and focus on the love they shared and the life they had built together.

But within a year of stopping their treatment, Sarita and Kanna's deepest wish was granted unexpectedly. Nature took its course and it surprised them in the most beautiful way— they were blessed with a baby girl.

"Pregnancy is nothing but a miracle," they often told themselves.

Shakthi was a brave and active child. Her birth was a turning point in Sarita and Kanna's life. She became the centre of their universe, healing their wounds with her innocent laughter. Thereafter, Sarita started finding new meaning and joy in her life. She resumed her job when Shakthi turned two, and Kanna's career also took a leap forward.

But as it is often said and seen, good hearts suffer the most, their happiness and peace didn't last long.

With a heartbreaking twist, a few years later, Shakthi lost her life in a road accident. The laughter and love that Shakthi brought into their lives now remained only as memories in a world that turned upside down for Sarita and Kanna.

• • •

Seasons passed, but the poor couple couldn't come out of their misery. Instead, they often found themselves lost in the thought of why they suffered for a baby and why she was taken away from them suddenly.

Over time, their well-being and happiness took a back seat. They held tightly to the precious memories of Shakthi. So as a result of their prolonged depression, Kanna started losing weight, and Sarita gained a lot.

But the couple paid little attention to their looks as they were immersed in the lasting grief. Especially, Sarita's brain hadn't yet processed the demise of her daughter. She loved her daughter to the core and now, she could not even touch her, see her, or feel her. And what haunted her more was not knowing the reason behind Shakthi's birth and death. On the contrary, her weight was just a minor concern to Sarita but sooner it became fodder for societal gossip. The community, ever so watchful, started judging them, passed a nasty comment and came up with an unsolicited suggestion to try for another baby. However, neither of them was liked by the couple instead, this only intensified their sufferings.

Now months turned into years, and the gossip wasn't just about Sarita's increasing weight. She began to have facial hair just like men. So, every time she stepped out of her house, hurtful comments like "Hey, look at her, she's got a moustache and beard" or "She's too hairy" wounded Sarita deeply.

Certain close relatives went to the extent of making fun of the situation, teasingly rubbing her chin and suggesting that she needed to try plucking, waxing, shaving, epilating, or anything that came off their mouth instantly.

People around Sarita were blind to the emotional chapters she was living. They saw only her exterior and chose to wound her with their focus on her hair. So, whenever someone embarrassed her by rubbing her chin, Sarita would get away from the hurtful environment immediately and she would run to her husband.

Kanna, as always, was the greatest support for Sarita. He used to pat her back, offering her strength and confidence whenever she hugged him tightly.

"Did they rub it again???"

Understanding Sarita's long hug, Kanna used to reassure her every time, "Listen to me, Sarita. Don't let their ignorance define you. It's a ridiculous social norm to say a woman's facial hair is abnormal. You will be ok when you come out of your stress."

Despite Kanna's kind words Sarita wasn't consoled as she could not tolerate the embarrassment she faced in public. So, at last, she ended up removing her facial hair for the sake of others.

But the more she tried, the more her hair became coarser and thicker. She also chose to have some laser hair removal sessions, but nothing gave her lasting results.

Frustrated, Sarita began feeling anxious whenever someone approached her in public as if she had committed a criminal offence. Eventually, unable to find a solution to her problem, she began covering the ingrown hairs and bumps with her hands whenever she went out. That's when Kanna decided it was time to take her to the doctor.

• • •

Upon arriving at the hospital, the couple was shocked to see a waiting room filled with women from all walks of life. They had the same issue regardless of their body type. As Sarita mingled with them, she discovered that more than half of the women confessed to regularly checking their faces in the mirror every three hours to hunt their ingrown hairs. "This became a habit now, causing a lot of mental pressure," they shared, the stress evident in their voices.

A few of them went ahead and voiced their experiences. "I don't see my hair as a big problem as I have it from my childhood, but now I don't go to family functions and get-togethers. I have been noticing since childhood that they only have one single thing to talk about me. Instead of asking how I am, they would ask me to seek parlours for my facial hair," a woman admitted. Another confided, "I decided to pluck only when my colleagues bullied me for my hairiness, otherwise I never felt this as a problem." Listening to them, Sarita realised that many of them were perfectly fine with their facial hair and their natural state—just as she has always been. It made Sarita recollect how facial hair never really bothered her, but it was the harsh lens of society that pushed her to seek treatment.

Further, along with the prescriptions, the doctor advised Sarita and Kanna to make some lifestyle changes which will help in lowering their stress levels.

Slowly, the couple took the doctor's words to their heart, incorporating changes into their daily routine to revoke them. Yet, the heaviness of those ongoing hurtful comments and rubs were still bothering Sarita.

It was during this period of adjustment, they received a call from Kanna's sister that brought a smile to their faces. Kanna's sister was coming to visit them, and the joy doubled for the couple when they learned she would be bringing her son Akhil along with her.

After a long time, a child was finally coming to their home. Sarita and Kanna, full of excitement, prepared Akhil's favourite sweets and snacks. They also brought down all of Shakthi's toys from the loft to give to Akhil. Although it was painful to remember Shakthi while cleaning the toys, they were happy to know that soon they would hear the giggles and playful shouts of a child in their home again.

They eagerly waited for Akhil's arrival…

• • •

Finally, Akhil came bursting through the doors and he raced into the arms of his aunt and uncle. He hugged and kissed them as he always did. Though it seemed a small gesture to the child, only the couple knew how precious the moment was. It was like a soothing balm to their aching hearts. Sarita and Kanna clung to him silently, their lips thanking the almighty until Akhil expressed his discomfort by kissing Sarita, "Are you having a beard, Sarita Aunty?" he said, his little hands tracing her face with childlike honesty.

With his innocent query, unknowingly Akhil reopened the wound Sarita had tried so hard to heal.

Sarita became conscious and upset after hearing the same question again, that too from a young child. But despite the surge of emotions within her, she masked her feelings with a smile, not wanting to hurt Akhil. Instead, she gently ruffled his hair out of affection and asked him, "Why didn't you mind kissing your uncle, even though he has a bigger beard than me?"

Akhil pondered momentarily and responded with a playful expression, "Only men should have a beard, Sarita Aunty, and you shouldn't. Look at my mother; she doesn't have one."

This time, it was exceptionally painful for Sarita to realise that a six-year-old boy's perception was already conditioned about how a woman should look.

Sarita remained silent as there were a lot of things running in her mind. Yet, she signalled Kanna's sister to stop scolding the child.

Further, Akhil and his mom spent three lovely days at Sarita's house and had a great time with the couple. As they were about to leave, Kanna's sister took Sarita to the backyard away from Akhil's earshot and with heartfelt regret, she said, "Please don't take Akhil's words personally. He is just a little boy."

Tears welling up in her eyes, Sarita responded with a surprising warmth. Holding onto Kanna's sister's hands, Sarita said, "Actually, your brother and I should thank Akhil. He is the one who answered our long-awaited question, 'Why did our daughter Shakthi leave us?' Kids don't judge; they imitate. Akhil honestly shared what he observes in society."

Sarita went on, her voice steady, "All these years during my journey with facial hair, I have interacted with many women who have the same problem for various reasons. Some had facial hair by nature, some gained it due to health issues. But every time, it's heartbreaking to witness how societal prejudice forces them to stay indoors. It almost feels like imprisonment, you know? But Akhil is the one who in a way pushed me to empower these women and help them embrace their unique beauty."

"I'm puzzled. How did Akhil contribute to this?" with a furrowed brow and a curious tone, Kanna's sister questioned Sarita.

"Akhil's words were like a wake-up call to me. He mirrored the harsh judgments of society. So, now, I have gained the courage and have made my decision to take the first step. Here afterwards, I'm going to face the world with this hairy face, no matter how I look or what anyone else thinks of me because only I know about the battles that I am fighting and the facial hair is a side effect of it. I'll not let any other child like Akhil be wrongly influenced by societal dictation of how a woman should look," Sarita said with confidence.

Hearing her bold words Kanna's sister became so emotional and proud. She immediately embraced Sarita with a tight hug, and while leaving, she took Akhil to Sarita and said, "It's normal for a woman to have a moustache like your aunt."

Sarita was visibly relieved and grateful for those kind words and support. And from that day forward, Sarita accepted her hairiness without shame. Both Sarita and Kanna made it their life mission to challenge societal taboos and boost the confidence of those facing similar struggles.

Even after many years of their decision, Sarita still faces nasty comments about her hairiness from both strangers and her circle. Yet, Sarita felt a sense of satisfaction whenever a woman with a similar problem admired her for her openness.

• • •

I didn't know Sarita until we met in a public place, where I encountered a confident and beautiful woman with a thick moustache and beard.

Sarita shared that they chose not to have a second child, realising that Shakthi came into their life with a purpose. Once they embraced this realisation and dedicatedly adhered to the doctor's advice, they became stress-free, and their weight issue was resolved soon. Sarita's thick hair didn't stop growing abruptly, but now she didn't bother about that.

Sarita and I had a meaningful conversation afterwards that spanned about various societal topics for quite some time. But I wish to end this narrative with what she wanted the world to know: "Never comment on anyone's unconventional appearance since we don't know what are the challenges they've been going through in their lives."

"Whether to keep it or shave it is a woman's choice, just like any man has," believes Sarita.

Evident eyes…

10

An Unplanned Journey

I often wonder, "Why do I call this place my second home...???"

I still remember the day I first arrived in Singapore. I had a lot of confusion and worries when I got to know that I would have to temporarily shift to Singapore. It was my first time in a foreign land. I was not sure how I was going to cope up in the country or how long I was going to stay there. But the very moment I landed on Singaporean soil I genuinely felt like I was reuniting with a part of myself that had been missing for a long time. On the other hand, surprisingly, the land seemed to recognise me as well! It embraced me with open arms, whispering, "Welcome back, my dear old friend."

Thereafter, I never felt like an outsider, never felt insecure or worried. In fact, that was the land where I shared a lot of sentiments and happy moments close to my heart. Moreover, the fact that my mother tongue, Tamil, was one of the official languages in Singapore deepened my connection with the nation even more.

From their sweetest local lingo "*lah*," "*leh*," and "*can! can!*" to the sense of security I felt while walking alone at night, I've adored everything about Singapore and its warm people.

As time went by, I slowly started my travelling journey across various regions in Singapore all alone. When it comes to exploring, though the island is commonly considered as small one, I must admit that Singapore is packed with wonders to discover. I have always had a distinctive approach while exploring the city-state—I never followed an itinerary. The thrill of not knowing what I'll find next has led to the most exhilarating experiences in my life than the pre-planned checklist ever did. So I always prefer unplanned journeys.

My weekdays were pretty much the same, finding bliss in my daily routine but weekends were transformative. I'd usually hop on public transport or rent a bicycle, along with my small yellow-coloured backpack—carrying a water bottle, lip balm, wallet, diary, and especially an umbrella as one can't trust the cloud's mood in Singapore.

• • •

It was one such weekend during a peak summer, I was getting bored at home and decided to step out for an adventure—I call them my solo dates.

As usual with no particular destination in mind, I took the first bus that arrived at the stop. It was heading to Woodlands, an area known for its lush greenery, diverse dining options, and shopping facilities. In fact, Woodlands is also well-known for its bridge connecting Singapore to Johor Bahru, Malaysia.

First things first, I bought 'Teh-C' (a common beverage in Southeast Asia, made with evaporated milk) in a random mall in Woodlands. For me, nothing says good morning like a cup of steaming tea. Feeling its warmth in hand and slowly sipping, I stepped out straight onto the streets of Woodlands, letting the city reveal its secrets to me.

Then I might have roamed around in the area for roughly two hours, striking up conversations with locals, capturing selfies, giving a pat to stray cats, and immersing myself in the lively atmosphere. Honestly, every street, every turn held a surprise for me in Woodlands—undoubtedly, each one drawing me closer to the country. However, as the sun climbed higher in the sky, the heat became unbearable, and I decided to continue my journey by bus—whichever comes first.

Well, it took a few minutes for the first bus to arrive. With each passing second, my curiosity went higher and higher thinking, "Where are you going to drop me off, huh? Perhaps that's the thrill of an unplanned journey," I said to myself.

Luckily, the first bus to arrive was going to Boon Lay. As soon as I saw the bus I became so happy as Boon Lay was another new area for me to explore. It would take approximately an hour to reach the destination but it didn't bother me much as my heart was looking forward to sweet suspenses.

I tapped the card and quickly found a window seat on the bus. For some reason, I have always felt like window seats were just made for me, or maybe I have been making an excuse to grab one. I plugged in my earphones and was lost in thoughts of Boon Lay—What would I eat there? How would the buildings look—modern or traditional? Where should I go first as I drop off? While all these things were running in my mind and with every tune of the song playing in my ears, the cityscape changed in sync outside the window and "Oh my god," it started raining as well. "What more could I ask for in a day!" I mused a silent celebration.

Rain has always been close to my heart, like a cherished lullaby that soothes the soul.

Since I grew up in a small village, rain was a signal for family gatherings during my childhood—a time of shared joy and laughter. As soon as we'd see the first drops falling, we used to rush outside and play. Especially, "*Mann Vasanai*", the earthy smell of wet soil, was like a therapy to us.

During that time, my brother and I used to play small games in the rain. The most common one was, that we would breathe in deeply the Mann Vasanai and then hold our breath contesting who held it for longer. We also had other silly games, like seeing who could catch the most raindrops on their hands, racing paper boats in the puddles, and creating funny dances as the raindrops splashed around us. The best part was not that; but the bets of our pocket money which were followed by those utterly stupid but wholesome games.

Those were moments of pure joy, and our bond with the rain made them even more special. But on that day, sitting on the bus, I missed those little games. Also, a pang of sudden homesickness hit me, longing to relive those carefree moments once again with rain.

"Oh! No! Why wait, Sara?" The little girl in me immediately consoled coming up with a remedy.

"Why not now? This is a signal to relive your childhood memories. Just get down and see what it has for you?" With that encouragement, I stowed my earphones back in their case and got ready to get down at the upcoming stop.

To be frank, on that day I just fully surrendered myself to the spontaneous flow of an unplanned journey—giving freedom to follow the heart and pause wherever it calls.

• • •

I got down at the next stop, feeling like the happiest person alive on Earth taking in the soul-stirring smell of Mann Vasanai. The air was so chill and the place was cool. Just like the little girl in me predicted I didn't know what was hidden for me at this stop. But when I started enjoying the atmosphere and was about to lose myself completely in the rain, my thoughts shifted towards food.

Good or bad, I have a unique relationship with hunger—it never comes calling until it's impossible to ignore. So, when my stomach started rumbling, I knew it was time to find food, otherwise, I'd be in trouble. Thus, I started looking for a nearby hawker centre, sadly disconnecting myself from the rain.

Hawker centres were my favourites in Singapore, one can get anything—from 'Nasi Lemak' to Thai 'Mango sticky rice' and fortunately, a quick glance at my map revealed one within close proximity.

To my surprise, the hawker centre was overflowing, it was more crowded than a usual weekend. Poor me, on one end I couldn't control my hunger and on the other end, I couldn't find a stall selling vegetarian dishes. Indeed, being a vegetarian was a challenge there. Moreover, the funny part was that I couldn't even find the difference between veg and non-veg since they all looked alike. So I started asking in every stall, "Is this a vegetarian dish?"

"Yeah Miss, we add vegetables in it…" I got mixed responses like this to the straightforward "No, that's fish," each one testing my patience.

Finally, after a few minutes of meandering here and there and making my enquiries, I discovered a stall selling food items suitable for me. "God hasn't forgotten me!" I chuckled and quickly ordered a customised hotpot, spring roll, and a refreshing iced lemongrass tea. Once I neatly arranged everything on a tray the next challenge was to find a seat while carrying a killing stomach.

Though some tables appeared vacant from a distance, as I approached, I noticed they were reserved with belongings like phones, bags, or other personal items—a testament to the safety and trust in Singapore. So, while carefully balancing the tray, I continued scanning for a few more tables but I didn't find any vacant ones.

At last, I was almost frustrated when I thought I'd have to eat standing. Yet, just when I was about to give up, like a beacon, I spotted it: an empty seat near the tray return area with a board, "Tray and Crockery Return". I immediately grabbed the seat before anyone would occupy it.

The hotpot looked incredibly tempting—its vibrant colours, brimming with fresh veggies and tofu, made it look absolutely delectable. However, when I took the first bite, it was seriously a trip to hell. The taste was a stark contrast to its delightful appearance and the high price I paid.

It was a huge bowl that I took and I didn't really want to buy anything else. After a few reluctant spoonfuls, I abruptly pushed the hotpot aside and started on to the spring roll. And oh! What a relief that crunchy spring rolls were; my stomach was satisfied after having them.

I am one of those people who takes time and feels everything to the core—be it a sip of tea, its aroma, rejoicing in the rain, spending time with colleagues in the office, or getting stuck in traffic jams. I feel that all of it makes me human, but this also makes me a keen observer.

So, on that day while devouring the spring rolls, I took in the lively scenes at the hawker centre—people from various walks of life were scattered everywhere. It was so nice to see kids darting in all directions and the lively air filled with chatter and clinking sounds. Yet, something was really off and interrupting my peaceful moments of savouring the food. I felt that someone was constantly eyeing me, casting a shadow over my enjoyment.

Initially, I dismissed it, thinking maybe that person just happened to look my way. But as the staring continued, I couldn't focus on my meal and was slowly getting irritated. As far as I knew, people in Singapore respected each other's personal space. Hence, this was making me uncomfortable.

Driven by a mix of curiosity and uneasiness, I slowly turned towards him. I wanted to know who that was and why he was constantly looking at me. But to my surprise, he wasn't the kind of person I was imagining, instead, he was an aged worker—looking fragile and diligently attending at the tray return station. So, after realising his age, "Okay, chill, all is well," I somehow got relaxed from the earlier discomfort but I still couldn't figure out the reason for his act.

"Hmmm, excuse me. What is this dish called?" All of a sudden my speculation was interrupted by a middle-aged woman with a beautiful Indian accent.

She seemed to be a tourist from India and she was eager to taste some local food there. So she hesitantly pointed to the hotpot before me and asked "Where did you get that?" Though I understood her eagerness, how could I suggest this dish to her? I could have talked to her a bit and informed her that this hotpot was so bad and that I wouldn't recommend it, but the aged man in the tray return area had all my attention, so I directed her to a different stall.

"Five stalls down, then turn right." It was a stall selling Indonesian dishes, located just opposite where I bought the hotpot. "Thank you, *Ma*," she expressed her gratitude and went to grab her food.

My attention then reverted to the aged worker once again. This time he was multitasking—along with organising trays, he was also cleaning up the spillages on the floor. In between, when he saw kids carrying the trays, he would stop mopping and move a few steps forward to help them. "Give it to me, I'll take that," saying with a soft assurance in his tone he received the trays from those children. And he seemed genuinely pleased when the bowls were empty. Yet he didn't fail to notice me quite often.

Now I got a bit confused about whether this man was good or bad because on the one hand, it was truly inspiring to see an elderly man with trembling hands going out of his way to assist others and on the other hand, I couldn't take his gaze lightly. "Enough is enough," I told myself and paused my meal for a moment to check him closely.

"Ohhhh!, now I got it! It was my mistake," only after carefully observing him, I noticed that his gaze wasn't on me alone; he was watching everyone around with equal attentiveness. It was a bit comforting to know that I was not alone. "But why's he watching everyone like that???"

Meanwhile, there came a bustling family, walking so fast and dirtying the recently cleaned wet floor. Their arms were full of trays cluttered with the aftermath of their feast—half-eaten chicken pieces, used tissues on top of a bowl of rice, and unfinished glasses of drinks. Though they interrupted the old man's cleaning work, it didn't dampen his welcoming demeanour; he greeted them with a warm smile, speaking of his years of service.

However, the old man's smile slowly faded when it was time to dispose of the leftovers. I saw a little sadness in his eyes but after taking a deep breath, he gathered all the waste and discarded it in the bin nearby. Then he went back to cleaning, unknowingly inspiring me.

I finally got it. After all the speculation I understood that his gaze was not intrusive at all, rather it was filled with concern for everyone eating there and every bowl of food. So I must admit that I misread his mind earlier.

Anyhow as time went by, the hawker centre became busier and busier with people searching for seats. I knew it was not nice to occupy a seat for so long. Respecting everyone's time, I resumed having my spring roll and iced tea. Once I finished, I cleared the spot and went to the tray return area.

There were four people queuing before me to return their trays, while I used the time to check the bus schedule to Boon Lay. My mind and heart were still synced in the symphony of rain, secretly wishing to experience it again that day.

The line moved swiftly, and it was finally my turn to return the trays. The elderly worker extended his hand towards me. He didn't say anything but looked at me for a fleeting second with a serious concern on his face. It was the same as the one I saw while he was gazing at everyone from a distance. However my brain was just thinking about the bus I had to catch, in four minutes, but suddenly it clicked for me—the reason behind his gaze.

"I'm sorry…I'm sorry.." I repeated, taking back my hotpot from his hands.

I knew no one was going to punish me for not finishing the meal, and saying sorry? may have looked unnecessary too. But I believe that was the right thing to do at that time because, at that very moment, his eyes genuinely took me back to my childhood memories—times when elders in my family severely scolded me once and taught me to value every single grain of food. As time passed by, I started earning and could spend on food easily so those lessons gradually slipped away from my mind. I used to buy a variety of food as much as I wanted to;

most of the time wasting it casually, if I didn't like it or if the quantity was more. Yes, that one glance made me feel like I was relearning those age-old simple truths of life once again. And I felt like a scared little girl standing before my own grandfather reminding me of the importance of food. I guess that's why Singapore feels like a second home to me, it has imparted lessons to me much like those I learnt in my homeland.

Once again after roaming around in search of a seat for a few minutes, I finally spotted an empty one. Whether I liked it or not, I finished the hotpot and came out of the hawker centre, saying, "Thank you, *thatha*," to the aged worker. "You are welcome," his eyes lit up with quiet recognition.

The term "*thatha*" might have been new to him, but certain sentiments need no translation.

• • •

It was still raining. Shortly, the next bus to Boon Lay arrived. I boarded the bus and found a seat near the window. I plugged in my earphones and started listening to music while looking out through the window and watching the beautiful cityscapes.

Now, along with the thrill of exploring Boon Lay, I felt a deep sense of happiness and contentment, realising the unplanned journey I had embarked upon, made a meaningful change in myself. This little one-day trip was not just about discovering new places, but about accepting the unpredictability of the journey and allowing myself to grow and enjoy the moment in unexpected ways.

An hour later, as expected, I got down at Boon Lay. It was another beautiful and captivating area of Singapore. I loved sightseeing and roaming its lively streets and shopping centres. Purchased some home decor, fries for snacking, and heels for myself. My joy was evident in the way my hands swung the shopping bags, doing a little happy dance.

As the day drew to a close, I was in the comfort of my home, trying on the new dresses I purchased from the mall. After all, I never end my trips without buying a dress!

On the whole, it was a perfect end to a perfect day. So, no matter how much one plans, it's the unplanned journeys that will always be in remembrance.

It shouldn't have happened to her…

11

The Perfect Pair

A few years ago, I got a pleasant surprise when my childhood friend, Mayuri, visited me. She came bearing good news that her wedding got fixed! I was so happy to see her after such a long gap and even more thrilled about her upcoming wedding. "That's wonderful, Mayu!", I said, hugging her tightly.

"What does your future husband do?"

With a hint of shyness, she replied, "He is in the construction business, based in Salem." "That's great," I responded, my heart filled with joy for her.

We then talked about many things and our conversation slowly turned nostalgic too, reminiscing about our shared past with laughter echoing in the room, just like old times. When we continued the discussion of marriage, I eagerly asked, "Do you remember them, Mayu?" She looked puzzled for a moment but then understood whom I was talking about and said,

"Ohhh! Them! The famous old couple, Sara? Azhagammai and Subbaiah from our village???"

"How can anyone forget the 'Perfect Pair'!" she exclaimed, and with that, we delved deep into our memories, discussing the iconic couple for the next few hours…

• • •

Azhagammai was a born beauty. In fact, that's why her father, Ranga, kept the particular name "Azhagammai", derived from the Tamil word *'Azhagu'*, which means beauty. However, her true beauty laid in her soul; she grew up as a gentle and kind-hearted girl with divine qualities. A girl who never knew how to hurt others, harbour jealousy, or let her beauty get into her head. All she knew was praying to Goddess Durga the whole day dutifully and doing whatever household task her stepmother, Valli, assigned.

Drawn by her beauty, once Azhagammai reached marriageable age, people from affluent families started approaching to wed her, but she remained humble.

Subbaiah, Valli's cousin—tall, dark, and handsome—was every girl's dream man. He lived a stone's throw away from Azhagammai's house and he was coming from one of the village's most reputed families.

Even though plenty of girls were ready to throw their hearts out for Subbaiah, his eyes were stuck on only one girl—Azhagammai. Right from his childhood Subbaiah was attracted by Azhagammai's beauty and his prime job every morning was to visit Valli's house as an excuse to see Azhagammai. However, when Subbaiah found out about Azhagammai's marriage proposals, he couldn't hold back his feelings anymore.

Subbaiah approached Valli and Ranga expressing his desire to marry Azhagammai. Since he was a well-mannered young man with clean habits, without further ado, Valli and Ranga agreed to the proposal and happily married Azhagammai to him with her consent.

Azhagammai was 16 and Subbaiah was 22 when they got married. After their marriage, Azhagammai didn't face any difficulty in Subbaiah's house, they all were kind people and took good care of her. Even though they didn't believe in gods, her mother-in-law respected Azhagammai's faith and bought her a big statue of Goddess Durga. And when Subbaiah's love for Azhagammai was concerned, no one could question it—she was one of the luckiest women to have found a caring partner like him.

Since Subbaiah and Azhagammai married at such a young age, they grew up together being friends rather than a typical couple. Always playfully teasing each other, fighting for small things and making up instantly, going out, cooking meals, and everything that friends do.

Moreover, when Azhagammai felt overwhelmed with household chores, Subbaiah didn't shy away from helping her out, even in the kitchen.

It was the time when men helping their wives with household chores were looked down on, but he never cared about what others were thinking and would roll up his sleeves to share her loads. Be it meal preparation, or a little task such as vegetable shopping, they worked as a team and it was their way of creating memories for a lifetime.

This bond made the couple the most favourite among villagers and a bit of jealousy for a few.

On the whole, their affection for each other was evident in every act, earning them the silent admiration of the villagers. However, the only hiccup was Subbaiah's frequent business trips, leaving Azhagammai at home. Nonetheless, she was always treated well by her in-laws.

Soon, they had a beautiful family of two daughters and a son. Though it looked like a complete and happy family, like any other couple, they too had their fair share of tough times in life. Despite that, their togetherness always won the battle, earning them the title of the "perfect pair" among the villagers.

A few years later, Subbaiah's parents passed away, he was then burdened with new responsibilities. He had to step into his father's shoes as the village headman along with a busy work schedule and ongoing business trips. While on Azhagammai's part, it was indeed an immense loss as she was very close to her in-laws. Both grieved the loss equally but the "perfect pair" with the blessings of the entire village, managed to handle the situation.

Once Subbaiah was appointed as the headman, his house became the go-to place for everyone in the village, where all matters, big or small, were counselled and resolved. Newlyweds would come to his house for blessings, believing their harmonious love life would be mirrored on their own. As years went by, they were no longer just the headman and his wife; they played the role of godparents for the entire village.

• • •

Time went unnoticed. Subbaiah and Azhagammai grew older. Their son, Sugumaran went abroad along with his family. Their daughters—Suryakala and Chandrakala, settled in nearby towns. But Azhagammai and Subbaiah refused to move anywhere because they both had an emotional connection with the villagers which was difficult to get detached from. They continued to stay in their century-old house, helping their people like they always did.

For many years, the perfect pair enjoyed a peaceful and loving life together, remaining an example to the entire village. But when Azhagammai hit sixty, their life took a turn.

Azhagammai started facing several physical health issues one after the other. However, the most painful reality was that her mental health also began to deteriorate. To everyone's shock, the woman, who once loved Subbaiah to the core turned arrogant towards him and she began shouting at him for no reason. Not only with Subbaiah, she used to sit on *thinnai*, to shout at passersby without realising what she was doing.

The poor Subbaiah was in turn shaken to the core, seeing Azhagammai's declining mental state. However, his love for her never changed, nor did he ever react rudely to Azhagammai's arrogant behaviour and hard words. Subbaiah cared for Azhagammai as one would for a newborn—feeding her, dressing her, doing everything staying by her side. "Azhagammai should be a gifted soul to have a husband like him," villagers wondered and felt happy for her that she got a pair who loved her selflessly.

Further, Subbaiah tried all possible means to recover his wife but his efforts went in vain.

• • •

Azhagammai passed away within a few months, leaving him all alone.

Undoubtedly, Azhagammai's death left a void in the village as well. The entire village mourned her loss deeply, but for Subbaiah, the grief was unbearable. He used to say that every nook and corner of their house, every sight in the village, wherever he went, reminded him of Azhagammai.

But the villagers didn't leave him alone and they left no stone unturned to bring him back as the headman.

Though he agreed to continue serving as the headman in the following years, Subbaiah became different now. Despite all the efforts by villagers, friends, and well-wishers, he could not smile like he used to, nor talk a lot. He lived each day with the hope of reuniting with his dear Azhagammai praying to her favourite Goddess Durga.

"This life is hell without you Azhagu. Take me soon." He was often found saying this and his words were very obvious to the villagers that he lost hope to live.

Years passed like this. His children would visit him occasionally and try to take him out with them, but Subbaiah remained with the loving memories of his dear wife. He continued his duty as a headman and looked after his business without a miss, and one day, he finally received his call, causing a heavy silence in the village. In every corner, in every conversation, there was a deep ache. It felt like the villagers had lost their very own father.

Subbaiah and Azhagammai weren't just two people; they were the heartbeat of the community. However, villagers believed and convinced them that the two pure souls—the perfect pair—had finally reunited in their afterlife. Perhaps, it was their way of comforting each other and ease their pain.

• • •

"Their life was like a beautiful poem, each stanza filled with love and togetherness, isn't it Mayu?" I shared my thoughts with my friend.

"Hmm…" Mayu replied in a thoughtful tone.

"On top of everything, I personally feel that Subbaiah's love and devotion for Azhagammai took an upper hand in their love story. Subbaiah was truly every girl's dream man." I concluded. But all of a sudden, Mayu became furious after hearing me and her reply was clear that she didn't share my sentiments or agree with my perspective.

"Oh! Please. Enough of this, Sara," her words were like a bitter pill to swallow. "A perfect pair is often an illusion," Mayu said with a sarcastic smile.

I was shocked and found it hard to accept her generalisation, especially when I had personally witnessed the profound love between Azhagammai and Subbaiah.

"Mayu, it's not fair to generalise based on a few imperfect relationships you might come across," I countered, trying to make her see my point of view. But it ended up triggering a heated argument between me and Mayu, the first in our long-standing friendship.

"Sara, what do you know about them? Subbaiah and Azhagammai, the so-called perfect pair, had a life that was far from perfect. Their life wasn't a fairy tale love story that you or the villagers believe it to be. Rather, it was a story of 'one-sided love and sacrifices', a saga that left a profound impact on the poor soul Azhagammai," Mayu's response silenced me.

"The culprit Subbaiah was a bundle of mere garbage, Sara, and a man of many faces…" Mayu began with a strong aversion towards Subbaiah.

"To the world, Subbaiah was a respected figure but behind closed doors, he was a wicked man. You might want to shut your ears hearing me, Sara, but I never mind, what I am about to tell you is the harsh unknown truth.

Subbaiah was not a man we all saw and admired. He was a womaniser and moreover, this was only known to his wife, Azhagammai. Can you imagine?"

My mind was baffled listening to her and I had no idea why Mayu was saying this. I had numerous questions running inside my head but I didn't want to interrupt her. Mayu continued…

"Subbaiah had a history of relationships with other women, a secret that Azhagammai discovered only after their marriage. A woman could bear anything in married life but cannot even think of her husband cheating by having affairs with so many women. Initially, the innocent girl Azhagammai tried to oppose and correct his ways but Subbaiah was a master manipulator. After all, it's always hard to deal with cunning minds, you know?

From the beginning itself, he never honoured his marital vows and never let Azhagammai express her emotions or voice her feelings, inside or outside their home."

"But they loved each other..." I attempted to interject Mayu, as the villagers had publicly witnessed their bond, which contradicted what Mayu was saying.

"Just let me finish. You will come to know the truth, Sara," Mayu cut me off without answering.

"Further, Subbaiah used his frequent business trips as a cover for his visits to other women and that was out of Azhagammai's control. He had Azhagammai in his house for society's sake, to maintain the good guy image, and also not to lower down his father's reputation.

In fact, he knew how innocent she was, and hence tried trapping her from the beginning. Going every day to Valli's house to meet her, saying sweet little things, and as soon as he got the opportunity, he married her. But all this was a big show. No wonder, Azhagammai had all the material comforts and outward appearances of a sophisticated, wealthy lifestyle after marriage, as expected of someone who tied the knot with Subbaiah's respected family. But she did not have inner peace in her home due to his mistreatment.

Then the poor Azhagammai, driven by the love of her children and to uphold her parents' happiness, chose to bear the burden of her husband's wrongdoings. Like many women, she kept these secrets to herself, protecting her family's honour and reputation.

Throughout their married life, Azhagammai endured Subbaiah's threats and deceit day by day. But despite the psychological scars, she maintained a facade of a happy and harmonious life for the public display.

As everyone in the village knew, when Azhgammai turned sixty, her physical health started falling. She then employed a nurse to assist her. But the fact that none knew was, one day, when she witnessed the sixty-six-year-old Subbaiah attempt to misbehave with her nurse, who was nothing less than her daughter, Azhagammai could no longer remain silent. It was all okay till his brutality was restricted to Azhgammai, but she could not see someone else suffering due to Subbaiah.

After many years of their marital life, Azhagammai found the courage to expose Subbaiah's real face and decided to reveal the truth before she died.

Azhagammai became impulsive and immediately called her daughters to tell them everything and warn them to be cautious after her death. But Suryakala and Chandrakala, who had blind respect for their father Subbaiah, refused to believe their mother's revelations. Not only them, but Azhgammai's son also dismissed her claims.

They all concluded that Azhagammai was suffering from age-related issues, causing her to falsely accuse their father. They sympathised with her and thought she needed extra care as this was turning into a mental illness. They further tried to convince Azhagammai that she was wrong about their father.

Though Azhagammai made several attempts to expose Subbaiah's other face, all her pleas fell on deaf ears. As days went by, the years of stress she had been silently enduring, coupled with her unsuccessful attempts to reveal Subbaiah's true character, took a toll on her mental health.

The poor lady began to lose control slowly, repeatedly accusing Subbaiah, regardless of where she was or who she was talking to. She would often sit outside her home voicing out the truth, "He is acting. Don't believe him," to anyone who would listen, or even to the empty air, but nothing worked in her favour.

Subbaiah, the heartless, selfish man took this as an opportunity to exploit the situation and portray Azhagammai as an unstable woman amongst the villagers. The villagers, due to their unwavering respect for Subbaiah, believed him. To be frank, it wasn't their fault either, because they had seen how well he behaved with Azhagammai in front of them. And who knows what was happening behind closed doors."

Mayu felt guilty for the villagers for blindly believing Subbaiah and then she continued the story, "Even today, it is hurtful to hear people say, '*Pavam* Azhagammai, she lost her mind. Such a fate shouldn't have happened to that good soul,' whenever they cross her house. But the truth was Azhagammai didn't lose her mind as they say, she was just fighting her own silent battles to expose Subbaiah.

A few months later, Azhagammai passed away but her heart was heavily burdened with unspoken truths. Anyhow, her death did not affect Subbaiah; he remained the same womaniser with his reputation untarnished.

His children took good care of him. He continued to live a long spotless life until eighty-seven years, respected by the villagers, while Azhagammai was remembered as the mad woman who dared to tarnish the image of her toxic husband," Mayu said the other side of the story, her voice cracked up and with tears in her eyes.

"But how do you know all these things, Mayu?" I inquired, my faith in her words teetering.

"The young girl who served as a nurse in Azhagmmai's house, was my cousin, Shobana. She used to work in a private hospital during the day and would visit Azhagammai's house every evening to assist her when Azhagammai's health faltered. As days went by, Azhagammai, in return, treated Shobana with kindness and began to regard her as her own child. That's why even after enduring bitter experiences at the hands of Subbaiah, Shobana continued her visits to their house. She was really unwilling to leave Azhagammai alone with such a brute. You know, Sara, Shobana was indeed the only person who truly listened to Azhagammai even when her own children failed to believe her," Mayu recounted.

"Azhagammai's last few days must have been filled with pain, isn't Mayu?"

"No doubt about that. It was heart-wrenching when Shobana described the pain in Azhagammai's eyes as she drew her last breath," Mayu confessed her emotions. She further added that from that day forward, she had lost faith in the concept of the "perfect pair" itself.

I kept quiet for a while after hearing Mayu. "Indeed, the perfect pair is meant to imply mutual respect and the willingness to make sacrifices for one another. But after hearing what has happened to Azhagammai, it seems the one who selflessly sacrifices and bears the burden of keeping the relationship intact ends up as the true loser." I said in a heavy choking voice a few minutes later.

"Remember, behind the facade of the perfect pair, there may be a tale of deceit and betrayal," Mayu said, wiping away her tears while she left on that day.

• • •

Ever since the last meeting with Mayu, whenever I hear someone describe a couple as the "perfect pair", I find myself questioning, who is the loser in their story? Is it Azghammai or Subbaiah?

First timers…

12

The Royals

I like slow Sunday mornings—getting up a little later than usual, having tea for myself and enjoying every sip before starting my routine. But that Sunday was different. I woke up, showered, missed my tea, and straightaway headed to the salon.

Though the salon was in the neighbourhood I took a few shortcuts to reach on time for my appointment. As I hurried along, I enjoyed noticing the typical Sunday morning scenes—men queued up in a lengthy line outside the butcher's shop, a few walking past me carrying a badminton racquet slung over their back, a person selling tea on a bicycle, a newsboy, and those closed shops depicting stillness of the day. But apart from all these scenes, my eyes were frequently drawn to a series of fluorescent posters stuck along both sides of the road.

Each poster had two images side by side, demanding the attention of any passerby. One was of a man with a villainous moustache and the other was of a woman with her high hair bun. Since I was in a hurry, I just cared less, thinking it was an over-promoted movie advertisement and I went ahead to enjoy my relaxing pedicure and manicure sessions.

But as soon as I entered the salon, literally everyone, from my favourite manicurist, Anu, to her apprentice Meena—was talking about the same fluorescent poster that I had seen a couple of minutes ago. For a while, I didn't understand what was so special about the poster and why they were super excited about it during working hours.

"Is it just me who didn't care about the posters?" I wondered.

"Can anyone tell me what that colourful posters are all about? Meena…? Anu…?" I asked them out of curiosity.

"What happened, *Akka*? Where were you? Why are you late? We've been waiting for you to come," Meena came up with a lot of questions. But before I could respond to her, she interrupted me, "Akka, let me tell you quickly. There's a great play going on and tickets are selling so fast now!" Meena said excitedly.

"Oh, now I got it," it was then that the fluorescent posters started making sense to me—the images I had seen were not from a movie, but a theatre play. Anyhow, I didn't really know that Anu and Meena were waiting for me to book the tickets.

Since I have been a regular customer at "Thara's Beauty Salon & Spa" I have developed a close relationship with the girls there, especially Meena, the sweetest one in the salon. She adores me a lot and treats me like her sister. We used to hang out quite often visiting restaurants and shopping malls nearby. But honestly, I have never been to any theatre play so far in my life and that particular day, I was not at all in the mood. I didn't want to spend the rest of my weekend wandering anywhere. So I remained silent for quite some time, not wanting to disappoint by refusing Meena.

Anu and Meena had back-to-back appointments in the salon after me, so Anu didn't wait for my response. She quickly started my pedicure and asked Meena to assist her. Yet, Meena didn't even move an inch from me until I said "ok" to her. She sat next to me and kept talking about the novel and the interesting facts behind it, which I listened to carefully but couldn't relate with.

"Alright, Meena, we will go today…"

Finally, we booked four tickets for the 6 pm play that covers all five volumes of the popular historical novel—Kalki's "*Ponniyin Selvan* (Son of Ponni)".

Meena was so excited and continued talking about the outfit and the matching accessories she wanted to wear in the evening until Anu screamed at her to do the job first.

Ponniyin Selvan is an ever-lasting tale of royal mysteries, romance, politics, and humour but, I hadn't read the book at that time. However, I remembered that we have a die-hard PS fan in our family—Renu, my cousin. I have heard Renu describe the beauty and intelligence of the princess character "*Kundavai Pirattiyar* (The Princess)" a zillion times during our summer vacations. Even upon graduating, she solo-travelled to the historical sites mentioned in the book to see the modern Chola dynasty. I thus thought of surprising her by taking to the show along with us.

Anu and Meena told me they would get permission from the salon and join us straight in the theatre at 5.30 in the evening.

• • •

I picked Renu up from her home and excitedly went to the theatre, which was 30 minutes away from our place.

We all went inside the theatre premises after Anu and Meena were formally introduced to Renu, but we didn't expect such a huge loyal fan base there. We stood in amusement and a little bit of surprise seeing the crowd.

The theatre was decorated more like a royal ceremony right from the entrance. Full of food stalls, inflated balloons, cotton candies, and gift shops selling PS t-shirts, stickers and other merchandise. Colourful photo booths and henna tents were also there. Meanwhile, we noticed a lengthy queue in front of the box office counter to buy the last-minute tickets, but the seats seemed to be sold out already. "Thank God! We bought tickets online," said Meena, taking a deep breath.

Since every stall looked so attractive and colourful, we stood there deciding which stall to check out first after watching the play. Even though we were running out of time for the play, the stalls caught our attention. "Let's put *mehendi* after the play," Meena suggested, pointing out the henna tents. "We will better buy the printed t-shirts first and then we can go to the henna tents," Anu and I said in unison.

Then we quickly took two to three selfies with the character cutouts in the theatre lobby and rushed straight to Hall - 02. We were awestruck seeing the stage design; it almost felt like we entered the Chola dynasty itself. Right from the detailing in the backdrop depicting ancient palaces and landscapes to the set properties, every element was thoughtfully designed to bring "Ponniyin Selvan" to life. So even though our seats were a little far from the stage we didn't bother as the stage design allowed anyone in the hall to clearly see the performance.

Within the next few minutes, the hall had almost reached its capacity with people of all ages. It was then that my eyes fell on him. If I'm not wrong, he must be in his early nineties. An elderly man wearing a white cotton shirt was being carried by his grandchildren from either side with great care. Though the frail man was unable to carry himself, I was surprised to see him holding a vintage edition of a PS book near his chest.

Further, I followed his actions and saw that he didn't put down his book even after taking his seat; perhaps it was not a book but an emotion.

The show was supposed to commence at 6 pm, yet no announcements were made about the delay until 6:30 pm. Initially, the audience waited patiently, but then they became intolerant and began shouting for an explanation when no one from the drama troupe showed up on the stage. And within the next ten minutes, the entire hall had transformed into a bustling fish market, with an angry audience demanding refunds and compensation.

However, amidst this chaos, there was a gentleman who remained cool and composed. He was the one who controlled the crowd with a mere hand gesture—striking palms loudly atop his head. It seemed like a different approach to all of us and it immediately caught everyone's attention. Inspired by his calm authority, all of us began to follow him and very soon the thunderous clap sound started echoing in the theatre. Moreover, we four had a blast clapping in sync and seeing each other's faces as we enjoyed the rhythm. It was truly unforgettable.

That was the first time I had witnessed such a creative way of controlling a potentially dangerous situation. His spontaneity not only controlled the ferocious crowd but also acted as a unique way of signalling the drama troupe that we all were waiting for their performance.

· · ·

We didn't realise how an hour passed. At around 7:30 pm, the host finally came on stage to make an announcement.

"Sorry for the delay and thanks a lot for your patience. We had an electrical issue due to heavy rainfall yesterday, but it has been resolved now. Here's your favourite period drama—Ponniyin Selvan. Please enjoy!"

Soon after he announced, the red pleated curtain was gently raised before us, and I can still recall the opening scene.

Absolutely worth waiting…!!!

Further, when the character "*Vallavaraiyan Vandiyadevan* (Warrior of the Vaanar Clan)" was introduced on stage, the audience started cheering in excitement—shouting, clapping, and whistling. But I had no idea who that was and why he was being celebrated. Still, I joined the crowd and welcomed him.

Renu and Meena seemed star-struck and couldn't take their eyes off him. But it was difficult for Anu and me to keep up with the twists, turns, and lengthy character names as the story moved on because we hadn't read the novel before.

Nevertheless, we were thankful to the artists who were portraying the characters "*Aditya Karikala Cholan* (The Prince)" and "*Nandini* (The Chief Antagonist)" because they were so good and in a way helped us to catch the flow.

Both performers maintained a consistent pace, seamlessly conveying emotions and delivering dialogues that captivated the audience. Along with the actual script, they also touched on a few sensational political matters in a satirical way infusing humour. Overall, they have created a positive and feel-good atmosphere, leaving us thoroughly entertained and engaged.

The show's first 45-60 minutes were so intriguing that time went unnoticed.

After that, there came a sea-based soulful composition, "*Alaikadalum Oindhirukka…*" sung by the character "*Poonguzhali* (a courageous fisherwoman)". Though the drama troupe didn't have the expensive sets or the facilities like a movie, they managed to master the song depiction as closely as they could. The wooden catamaran, music, and lighting effects were created under a dark sky with simple equipment. I might have missed the visual feast if Meena hadn't compelled me in the morning.

The performance continued to be awesome, and there was not even a bit of lag or a sloppy scene anywhere in between.

. . .

He was the one who started everything.

A middle-aged man, exactly at a point when the audience was undergoing the great turmoil of the sensational murder of Aditya Karikala Cholan, he didn't mind slurping something loud and tasting his crunchy potato chips open-mouthed, knowing that the entire grieving hall could hear him. At one end, the performers were trying to give their best to portray the mysterious scene "Who killed Karikalan?" as emotionally as possible, and at the other end, that middle-aged man continued crunching and munching, without caring about the performers or those sitting nearby.

Although snacks and soft drinks are not something uncommon in a theatre, he forgot to realise that, it wasn't a movie screening and he wasn't in his living room.

Though his act distracted the performers and irritated a set of audience like us, I don't know how some people in the audience found his actions tempting. They also started unwrapping their noisy packages and gave him company. Soon, the entire theatre hall smelled of crispy chicken wings and fried potatoes. Despite being hurt, the artists on stage didn't show it on their faces. They kept their emotions under control and continued their performance to not cause an unpleasant situation for everyone else who were genuinely interested in the play. However, there is always a thin line between annoyance and disrespect; what is acceptable and unacceptable.

In the very next scene, a family of four sitting in the front row, abruptly exited the show, possibly by an emergency call as they anxiously spoke on the phone. But even before the family reached the exit door, a woman I was sharing my armrest with, rushed to occupy those vacant seats in the first row. She was then followed by her husband and son, disturbing many.

Soon after they moved, their seats were filled by the young boys from the back. And the rupturing chain of moving forward and seeking a better seat continued. However, some of us were still glued to our seats and tried taking stage peek-throughs in between the floating crowd. At last, big fights broke out when the thin line of the boundary was crossed by walking on others' feet. Including Renu, many other fans had raised their voice for the unacceptable behaviour.

"Renu, performance is still going on. Calm down, at least for the sake of the artists, please…" I tried to soothe her. Since she couldn't take the annoying things happening inside the theatre hall, like many other loyal fans, Renu also walked out.

I genuinely had no clue how to console her.

Three of us rushed behind and tried to take her back, but Renu refused to enter the hall again. Her words were firm and furious.

Renu was basically a calm and composed person, and I had never seen her behave that furiously anytime before.

"She is right; there is no point going back. They have already abused the beautiful play enough. Let's go home," Meena was also equally hurt. But I personally wanted to watch the last few scenes of the historical play, still, I didn't force them. As Meena said, there is no point in going back.

Our plans of buying PS t-shirts and going to henna tents were completely shattered as we weren't in such a mood and we wanted to head straight home instead.

Anu and Meena took a cab to their room, and after sending them off, I went to the congested parking lot to find my two-wheeler.

Renu sat behind me without even saying a single word. I know she was deeply hurt. So, I gave her some time to deal with her emotions alone, but she didn't seem to be getting relaxed. "That's okay, Renu. Forget it. It's not our day," I started the conversation to break her silence, yet she didn't respond to me immediately. Understanding Renu and her love for the novel, I gave her some more time to come out of the disappointing incident.

Even though she took a long time to voice out sitting back, it was very intense and heavy once she opened up. That's when I understood the depth of her silence—"I am not upset about someone walking on my feet or my favourite novel getting spoiled, Sara. It's all about the on-stage performers and the dying ancient art."

When she said "dying art," I finally grasped her true pain. It wasn't the chaotic crowd that upset her; it was their disregard for the art she cherished.

"You know what, the number of audiences coming to the theatre shows has been largely reduced due to changing technology and social interest nowadays. Only a few troupes are still putting their shows on with a determination to pass the legacy to the next generation, and that's not at all an easy job," she continued.

"It takes a team of professionals, including makeup artists, lighting technicians, and support staff, to bring a production to life. The troupes have to pay at least a minimal remuneration to every one of them. That's why I immediately agreed when you called me in the morning. You know how much I love Ponniyin Selvan. I was really happy to see the overflowing audience, but what's the purpose of coming to the show when they forget why they came? Neither they enjoyed the performance, nor did they allow others to. At least the tickets could have been given to those who deserved them. Moreover, if people keep causing such chaos and disrespecting actors, how will this art grow, Sara?"

"That's true…" I replied.

Renu then continued talking about many things happening behind the screen to put on a show. Including me, most of the audience who came there never knew the other side of the theatre shows, which Renu was talking about. So, I didn't stop Renu until she unloaded all her emotions, but after that, I wanted her to clarify one unsettling thought that I had.

"Then why did you leave the show before it ended, Renu? Don't you stand in the same line as those who distracted the performers?"

"I do not know if what I did was right or wrong, Sara. I kept my calm for a long time but there is a limit to everything. I didn't have such a strong heart to be there when the performers were insulted by their very own audience. Who knows, the person who did the cameo might have been awarded a lead role in his next show. His performance deserves that, but he went unnoticed while people searched for better seats. His nerve-wracking audition, late-night rehearsals, long hours of makeup, and every other effort to give his best were greatly insulted, and his opportunity was buried deeper. Just imagine how painful it should have been for him.

And not just him, Sara. Like I said, there are many people involved in the play, this chaos could take a toll on anyone's career and refrain them from further opportunities. After a lot of effort, they bring up such performances on stage and if that too is disrespected to this extent, then we fail as an audience. That's why I became furious and left the show. I'm sorry you missed those ending scenes."

What Renu said was one hundred percent right. I don't think it requires a three-year bachelor's degree to teach the basic theatre courtesy for the so-called modern minds—Put your mobile phones in silence for a few hours, do not pass mid-show commentaries, stay away from rustling packages, or be sensible at least. And most importantly, never try to find a better seat once the show commences.

As Renu said, a breach of these theatre etiquettes had surely insulted and distracted the live performers.

• • •

At last, we reached home and had a strong cup of coffee together. I asked Renu to stay at my home for that night and I would drop her off the next morning.

Once she agreed, I watered all the plants in the backyard and proceeded to cook her favourite dish—*Masala Dosa*. While cooking, I tried to keep her entertained by sharing some of our childhood memories, but she seldom laughed.

Renu remained silent and unsettled even after we went to bed.

It was around 1 o'clock in the night and she was still awake, worrying and talking about him—The Frail Man!

"Will he get another chance to watch a live performance in his remaining days, Sara? He might have been a person who selflessly worked for the welfare of his family throughout his life and all that old soul wanted was to fulfil his very own small wishes, like watching his favourite play before he reached his final destination. Knowingly or unknowingly, everyone in the hall shattered his wish, didn't we?"

"Honestly Renu, I have no answer for you, but I hope he sees the show somewhere else again. Now, don't hurt yourself, close your eyes," I strictly told her.

Since I was tired, I immediately fell asleep, but Renu was awake for a long time, praying for his wellness.

In our fast-paced lives full of fleeting encounters, none of us have time to slow down a bit to even think about what the other person is actually feeling. Especially with strangers. But that day watching my cousin grow up as a pure soul brought tears to my eyes. Her deep concern for the artists and the frail man truly made me feel guilty for not thinking like her—She was praying for the frail man, while my selfish concern, as her sister, was only to calm her down and put her to rest.

I knew one thing for sure: at that moment, there was nothing I could have said that would have helped her to feel better. So, I gave her some water and asked her to sleep. After a while, drained from thinking about the incident, she slept. "I'm proud of you, Renu," I whispered when she closed her lids.

. . .

Undoubtedly Renu's kind heart made a strong impact on me and from that incident, I see a Renu inside me whenever I am with others, especially in theatres. And I swear, every time I could feel the emotions of others, just like Renu did. Now, I feel much more satisfied and good about myself.

"Thank you, Renu, for making me feel more human now."

That's how I shop…

13

The Day I Met Durga

I used to spend a lot of time at my grandmother's home in a small village in Tamil Nadu. My grandmother, Irulayi, was the most compassionate and beautiful woman I have ever seen. Though my grandma had more than ten grandchildren, I was her favourite. She knew how much I loved *kuzhi paniyaram* (a golden brown, bite-sized South Indian snack made from fermented rice and lentil batter) and would prepare it, especially for me every time I visited her. I still remember, my grandma used to cook paniyaram on a traditional "Firewood Stove" and I would assist her in picking wood sticks. In fact, these small things were what made us bond together strongly.

Apart from that, my grandmother would also tell me many mythical and short stories which usually started with, "Once upon a time, there lived a king and queen…" to keep me engaged while she cooked paniyaram.

Stories like "Arjuna and his Gandiva" and "The Greedy Merchant" were the best of all, and I insisted on repeating them daily. My grandmother was an excellent storyteller, her unique narrations always made me drown in an imaginative world. In fact, she made the characters come alive in front of my eyes. On the whole, time spent with my grandmother always felt like a magical fairy tale. Even now when I turn back, those were my life's most peaceful and carefree days.

Tuesdays were extra special for me, it was as if the whole week saved its best surprises for that day.

The villagers used to take off to go to *sandhai*—a nearby village market to buy vegetables and groceries for the upcoming week. So, on Tuesdays alone, my grandmother would start preparing paniyaram early in the evening, making me sit aside but close to her and telling me fascinating stories.

As soon as she finished preparing paniyaram, we would start getting ready, and I was always the most excited one. She would quickly wear a roughly pleated cotton saree with a big bindi adorning her round face, and dress me up in a long skirt and a matching blouse. We'd then grab two wire bags, big and small, hanging in the storeroom and head to sandhai walking side by side.

Though it was only a brief ten-minute stroll to the sandhai, she used to tell me stories all the way down. This time, they weren't the usual mythical stories; they were about her sandhai experiences.

She would proudly and repeatedly mention that the sandhai in her village was the biggest and one could buy anything from there—from wool to wooden rope cots. "Grandma, I have heard this many times earlier from you," I would funnily remind her and insist on telling my all-time favourite stories but she was so into the sandhai culture that she would never listen to this request of mine.

Moreover, her sandhai stories included all the processes that took place to set up the sandhai—the sellers would come early in the morning and start arranging their wares under the colourful tarpaulin shelters to protect them from the sun and rain. "And then, once it was all set up by the sellers, the villagers would rush to buy groceries and fresh vegetables, *Kannu*," she would finish, her voice tinged with affection for her village.

However, my grandmother and I would prefer to go to sandhai in the evenings to avoid the rush. Grandma's main reason for visiting sandhai was good quality and fresh vegetables, but my little heart just craved indulging in mini onion samosas sold by *Ammani Atthai* at the end of the street.

• • •

Once we entered sandhai, she would first get me the samosas to keep me quiet, and then she would proceed to buy vegetables. Grandma always followed a certain pattern of buying the necessities. She would start with a kilo of small onions, yet she never bought them immediately, instead, she used to wander the whole sandhai and inquire about the rates from all the sellers. Sometimes, amidst discussing rates, they would exchange casual conversations, asking about each other's health, medications, and recent family visits.

In the meantime, when I had nothing to do, I used to live in my own world of enjoying mini onion samosas and observing what the cobbler was doing; how the knives were sharpened or how the old vessels were polished until she returned.

Finally, after finishing her rounds, she would return to the seller who offered good vegetables for a lower price dragging me from my little explorations.

In sandhai, most of the sellers kept a slightly higher price for the vegetables and fruits, knowing that the buyers would bargain. Thus, my grandmother used to negotiate with the seller until they agreed to the price she had in mind. During this process, I would patiently wait, holding her hand with the expectation that we would buy the vegetables and go home soon.

Nevertheless, in some shops, when the seller was unwilling to reduce further, even after minutes of bargaining, she started walking away. And that was one of the most frustrating moments for me as a child. "Grandma, it's tiresome to even consider moving to the next shop and bargain once again. Why don't you buy it in this shop itself?" I always wanted to tell her, yet I couldn't.

However, when I had ample visits to sandhai with her, my grandmother's move became obvious to me. Every time we took a few steps, the seller would call back and offer the vegetables for the same price she wanted. "What?! You are rocking grandma," I said with a long smile because she managed to close the deal for one-third of the price the seller initially quoted. Nevertheless, she has always been respectful towards those sellers and hence they also treated us like a small chosen family, even after the bargaining session.

Not only my grandmother, but I have also encountered men and women from neighbouring villages who bargained in the same way to save their hard-earned money in sandhai. They always made sure to get the best quality at the lowest price.

Moreover, the beauty of bargaining in those days was that both the buyer and seller haggled with smiles on their faces as if they'd known each other for ages. As far as I remember, I never saw a bargaining session ending up in a heated argument, one of the parties would simply give up on the other.

Back then as a small girl, witnessing villagers saving money while maintaining mutual respect intact made me understand that bargaining is an art and it is an integral part of every common man's life in India.

All in all, I cherished the ritual of going to sandhai which was filled with bright colours, enticing aromas, and unfiltered people. However, those cheering moments came to an abrupt halt when my beloved grandmother, the one who introduced me to the magic of the sandhai, passed away. It's as if a piece of my childhood was forever silenced and I never went to sandhai after her.

"I miss you, Grandma…"

• • •

Many years later…

I went to Chennai to search for a job after finishing my bachelor's.

My friends and I chose to stay in a women's hostel in a prime location to look for jobs. Those days, we used to attend a lot of interviews throughout the week, often causing us to miss our breakfast and lunch. Yet, we didn't get the right job for a long time and we got frustrated a bit as time went by.

That was the time one of our roommates, Meghna, an IT professional, suggested a different perspective. "Don't stress yourselves, girls. Take a break from the job hunt," she advised. "Go and explore some shopping streets that might lift your spirits."

"Where shall we go, *Akka*?" I asked her to suggest a place as we were new to Chennai.

"Better go to Ranganathan Street, the neighbourhood of T. Nagar. You will feel relaxed witnessing the craziness of the place," she recommended and further insisted that, "it's a must-go place when someone comes to Chennai."

Meghna Akka sounds right and I became excited after hearing her but my friends kept ignoring her suggestion as they didn't want to deviate from the job search. However, a few weeks later, all my friends went to their hometowns to celebrate Diwali, one of the biggest festivals in India. Since I was alone and idle in the room, I considered that a good chance to explore the Street.

With a sense of eager anticipation, I started from my room with a water bottle and an umbrella—the companions of my adventure as always.

When I entered the Ranganathan Street, it looked more like a *mela* since it was nearing the grand festival, Diwali. Both sides of the noisy stretch were jam-packed with shops and hawkers selling everything—from footwear to hair extensions. The best part was all the items were priced far cheaper than in other shops in the city, perhaps that's why it attracts a lot of people.

But I wasn't amazed by the craziness of that vibrant street, as Meghna Akka had described. Instead, I felt so connected and happy after so many years, since it brought back the precious memories of going to sandhai, tightly holding my grandmother's hand. So, basically, the street with the highest revenue yields in Chennai looked like a modern sandhai to me.

Even though I didn't buy anything from the shops over there, I kept meandering through the street for almost half of the day as I used to roam in sandhai—enjoying the simple pleasure and observing what people were doing there.

In no time, the bustling Ranganathan Street became a part of my regular weekend routine.

• • •

Every Sunday turned into my "me time" as I started going to the Street all alone.

Interestingly, the very next week, when I stepped down from the Mambalam railway station—the gateway to Ranganathan Street, my senses were immediately drawn to a familiar sight—a basket full of mini onion samosas—just as it was in sandhai. To my surprise, it resembled the same size and gave off the delicious aroma that I experienced in my childhood.

"Oh! You are here," I exclaimed after seeing those cute little ones. And of course, I wanted to have them immediately. I went near the man who was selling them and inquired about the price, "*Ithu evvaḷavu, Anna.*"

"5 for Rs.10, *Ma.* You want it?" Samosa Anna's response made me even more excited as the price was affordable. Yet I didn't buy them.

The excitement surged through me, but it quickly collided with a sense of responsibility. Since I was jobless and living off my mother's money, I felt guilty about spending on anything which wasn't absolutely needed at that time. So, I controlled my temptation and made a promise to myself, moreover consoling myself, that I would have those crispy delights only on the day I received my first salary—savouring each bite without guilt.

Thereafter, I started counting down the days until I could have them.

Even though every day I was craving mini onion samosas, I didn't want to fail myself. I tried a lot to get a job as soon as possible but honestly, the quest for a job wasn't smooth and the day I eagerly awaited didn't come that easily.

Around the time I graduated, a lot of students in India also completed their engineering degrees, and we all were running a rat race. The competition was intense to get a job. But good things come to those who wait. I ended up getting a job next to the Street I loved walking through.

"What a great twist!" I felt so lucky. Now, I could cross the Street twice a day instead of only on weekends.

From the first day of my job, I made sure to start a little early from the women's hostel so that I could really take in the slow life of Ranganathan Street while crossing it. Perhaps it was my way of connecting with a nostalgic pulse—soaking in the morning sights and sounds of Ranganathan Street; watching the shopkeepers open up the shops and start their day and trucks unloading materials.

Since the Street was a little empty in the morning, the shopkeepers used to call me by shouting, "Offer! Offer!", "*Vanga amma, vanga*", in the hope that I was a possible buyer while I walked through slowly. However, I would just flash them a friendly smile and move on as I knew I was not going to buy anything.

Once again, in the evening, after finishing my work, I used to walk on the same street reading the chalkboard menu in the ice cream parlour, looking over the colour combinations of the beautiful *bandhani dupattas* swaying outside some nameless shops and finally pausing to eye the mini samosas in a corner. But the street was never as silent as it was in the morning; from one end to the other, I was pushed by the crowd behind me, turning my walk into an adventure.

And that was my routine for the next thirty days, each day bringing me a step closer to that much-anticipated moment— the arrival of my first month's salary.

• • •

Finally, the long-awaited day had come—the day I'd treat myself to those mini samosas I'd been eyeing.

It was a Friday, and I was buzzing with excitement. As soon as I stepped into the office, I was glued to my phone, eagerly checking for that notification—"Your salary has been credited." Perhaps I was the only one who looked forward to the salary to savour mini samosas, while others were anxious to settle their EMIs. But to my disappointment, at the end of the day, I was only given a "cheque" worth Rs.5,500. "Seriously??? No, this is not happening," I told myself, stepping out of the office with a mix of humour and disappointment.

I had no other choice then but to count the days with patience.

When my cheque finally cleared after a few days, the thrill of samosa day was real! But before I could rush out, my first instinct was to take a moment to wisely divide up my earnings—"A good budget is the best seasoning for any treat," I thought.

First, I set aside Rs.5,000 for my hostel rent, which covers the basic needs: food, electricity, and laundry. Once that was sorted, I only needed to think about my seasonal train pass, costing roughly Rs.100 back then. After these, I was left holding four hundred-rupee notes in my hand which actually made me feel rich for a moment.

Even though my earnings weren't much at that time, I was so happy that finally, I could take care of my needs on my own.

Indeed, something from within was urging me to buy as many crispy samosas as I needed with the balance money.

Like my mother always taught, I made sure to keep some money for savings before spending the rest. So I saved half of it in a hidden zip inside my handbag before approaching the man selling mini onion samosas on the street corner.

The moment I got five samosas wrapped in an old newspaper, I couldn't hold back. I started gobbling, even before the seller handed me my change. Of course, my mouth got burnt after eating the first samosa in a hurry. So, I decided to go to a spot that was less chaotic and I slowly began to eat the second one. Now, I could relish; it was perfect, and even the proportions of onion and potato were also the same as the ones I got from sandhai.

When my taste buds started realising the same taste after many years, goosebumps ran all over my body. For the first time after a long while, I felt a familiar energy around me, as if my grandmother was somewhere nearby. The crispy onion samosas—for which I had been craving for the past thirty days, something that was supposed to bring joy, suddenly turned out to be a reason for utter grief. I took another bite, but couldn't chew it properly as tears rolled down my eyes. I started looking around with a childlike curiosity, searching for my grandma's presence.

I was sure that the inexplicable feeling was not my imagination but soon reality struck me and I wiped my tears. I kept the remaining three samosas in my handbag to give to my roommates so that they could savour it without pulling any heartstrings.

I then felt okay after drinking a sip of water, and I went ahead to buy something for Shruti.

Shruti was a good friend of mine, she was the one who referred me for the job that I might not have known about otherwise. So, as a token of appreciation for her help, I wanted to buy her something special.

As far as I know, Shruti likes *dupattas* a lot, especially bright-coloured ones. Therefore, I decided to buy a bright bandhani dupatta for her.

I approached several sellers, inquiring about prices, but I didn't make a purchase immediately. Just like my grandmother, I was quite cautious while spending my hard-earned money and also worried about getting ripped off by shops that charge unreasonable prices. Hence, I took my own sweet time and went from one shop to another inquiring about prices.

Surprisingly, they were all open to bargaining, similar to the sellers in sandhai.

Finally, after wandering the whole street for an hour, I was attracted by a beautiful bandhani dupatta, which was fluttering next to a small tailoring unit, carrying a board, "Get your *salwars* stitched in an hour."

The particular seller didn't have a separate shop or a pushcart to sell her wares. Instead, she had strung all the dupattas on her shoulder using a long pole standing near the tailoring shop. She had almost all bright colour dupattas and was attractive too.

The red one hanging as the last on the pole caught my eye, so I pointed to it, asking, "What's the price of that red dupatta, Ma?"

The seller replied to me but what she quoted was thirty rupees more than the others, and at that point of time, Rs.30 was a huge amount for me. However, I wanted that particular design, hoping Shruti would like it. So, I didn't negotiate for a lower price but a fair one with the seller.

"*Peram pesama idatha gali panu,*" she immediately became angry and yelled at me to leave the place if I wanted to bargain. That was a really harsh response, and I didn't see any other seller behaving in such a way on that street.

I felt so humiliated, "Fine. Keep your dupattas with you," I said and left the place.

Since I'm a sensitive person it took a few minutes for me to get back to normal before I could approach another shop for the same colour dupatta. But as I neared the next shop, she started following me and requested to buy her piece.

Initially, I ignored her and moved a few steps thinking she would stop coming behind but she didn't. Instead, she started coming wherever I went. Her persistence made me feel uneasy and a little afraid too. So I walked fast towards the shop, "Sorry, Akka," she stopped me in between and quickly grabbed my wrist. She apologised for yelling at me.

After hearing her apology even though a part of me warned that it could be a trick to make people buy sometimes, being called "Akka" melted me a bit. I took a deep breath and turned to politely decline her dupatta.

"No one has bought even a single dupatta since 5 pm, Akka," she looked so pitiful and innocent while saying that. "Everyone inquires about the price and leaves; that's why I behaved so harshly with you," she said and didn't even wait for my reply to say sorry one more time. Her justifications didn't convince me to accept her rudeness but I started feeling sorry for her. I couldn't ignore her dupatta after seeing her wet eyes.

"I'll buy your dupatta, don't worry," I assured her, finally making the decision to buy. I thought she would be happy after hearing me but she wasn't. Instead, she seemed restless and anxious to sell all her dupattas before it got darker. Obviously, I can't buy all of them and I couldn't figure out why she said that. But I was sure that something was disturbing at the back of her mind.

"Are you hungry?" I asked to pacify her first. She didn't answer my question, but her quiet refusal spoke volumes, revealing both her hunger and self-respect.

I immediately reached into my bag and handed her those three samosas and water. Although the samosas did not completely satisfy her hunger, she felt relaxed a little after eating. "I never sold dupattas in this street earlier Akka, that's why I do not know the right price or how to behave with a buyer. This is my father's business, and he never allowed me to see him on the Street for some reason. He always pushed me to study well," the seller explained, her voice laced with a longing for understanding.

"Oh. What do you study?"

"10th class. But for the past two days, I've been juggling my studies and my father's business since he has been hospitalised," she continued to vent out all her emotions.

"But despite his illness, my father was confident that he would recover and stressed me to study well till then."

"Then why did you come here? Why don't you concentrate on your studies?" I asked out of concern.

"Akka, though he tries to console me, I could see the truth—his health is deteriorating day by day. I don't want to be a burden; I want to support him and take care of our expenses on my own here afterwards. That's why I came to this street, without telling him. But, you know something? Although the street looks colourful all day, it doesn't for a girl like me as it gets darker. I am still afraid after being harassed last night."

Her last few words hit me hard but I kept my reaction to myself and tried to boost her up. It seemed even though she was a small girl, she was dealing with huge things. Her fear of harassment, fear of eviction from the Street, fear of losing her father, or giving up her education really bothered me a lot.

At last, I was shocked to hear that she had been talking to me for the past few minutes in the urge to use the toilet, but there was no hygienic toilet facility. As a female, I could relate to every other thing she had shared with me. But, being a young woman myself and not financially strong, I was unsure how to assist with all her problems.

I then requested a person in a shop nearby to take care of her wares and took her to a big store at a walkable distance to use the toilet. At first, she hesitated to get inside as she felt that she was not wearing a good dress as others. But I didn't mind, I gently grabbed her hand and led her to the toilet to use it without feeling conscious. "Trust me, you will also open a big store like this one day," I told her while we were returning to collect her wares.

If I had enough money, I might have bought all her dupattas without even thinking for a second. But that day, I could buy only two, investing the money I had put aside for my savings. Further, I promised to meet her regularly while returning from the office to give moral support.

"Thank you so much for those kind words, Akka. I'm feeling relaxed now," she expressed with a sigh of relief. "I'm also equally relaxed after meeting you and sharing sentiments," I responded to her wholeheartedly.

Both of us then parted ways, waving goodbye, after immersing in an unknown bond that had quietly woven itself between us.

"Akka…" As I moved a few steps, she called me again with a curiosity to know my name. "My name? Oh! I didn't say that?" I laughed.

I told her my name but deep down I always wanted Durga to call me "Akka".

"I'm your elder sister, now and forever okay?" I told her, my voice filled with a sisterly command and her naive smile made my day.

· · ·

It's been more than ten years now. Whether the extra thirty rupees Durga asked for was right or wrong, the day I met Durga was the last day I bargained; she made me realise that I would be bargaining with someone who was trying to make a living with that very money.

Share with Us

I greatly value your thoughts and would genuinely love to hear from you. Have any of these stories touched your heart? Or perhaps was there a moment that made you pause and reflect? Your feedback really matters to me, and every voice counts.

Moreover, if you have a real-life story that you believe could inspire others and you're open to sharing it with the world, I invite you to send it to us. Remember, every story has the power to inspire. Your story could be the catalyst for someone's transformation and might be featured in the upcoming books.

Excited to hear from you!

Write to us: writer.saranyaem@gmail.com

Acknowledgements

I've been fortunate to receive the backing and encouragement of many amazing people throughout the journey of creating this book. It wouldn't be possible without them.

Firstly, to the souls who breathed life into these pages—your stories are the heartbeat of this book. A big shout-out to everyone who has been an inspiration. "You've touched my life in ways you may never know, and I'll be forever grateful to you all."

To my father, **Mr U.P.Murugesan**, who is no longer with us. My father was the most ethical and righteous person I have ever known. He was the one who taught me to dream big and to live a meaningful life. "Thank you for being my guiding light, Daddy."

To my mother, **Mrs Selvi Murugesan**, a woman I've always looked up to. I owe her an immeasurable debt of gratitude for her unconditional love. Without her, my life would have lacked direction midway. "Your love and support mean a lot, Ma."

To my uncle, **Mr Jagadeeswaran Natesan**, who has been a steadfast pillar during difficult times. "I will always be deeply grateful to you, Uncle."

A heartfelt thanks to my brother, **Mr Saravanan Murugesan**, who has always been there for me like a fatherly figure. His honest feedback and constant support have been instrumental in shaping this book, "I love you and respect you to a great extent, Sarna." I also want to express my thanks and love to his dear wife, **Mrs Sudaroli Saravanan**, whose kind words have been a source of encouragement, "Thank you for spreading positivity, Sudar."

A special note of thanks to my dear husband, **Mr Murugan Sankar**, the most handsome and lovable man. He was the first one to learn about my writing and has been my biggest cheerleader since then. His faith in me was immediate and unwavering but I'm extremely sorry for disturbing you by always asking, "Hey, can you read this now???"

I extend my gratitude to my in-laws, **Mr Sankar Ekambaram** and **Mrs Geetha Sankar**, for their blessings and support. I can still clearly picture the genuine happiness on their faces when I revealed my plans to write a book. "Thank you Ma & Pa from the bottom of my heart."

Next are my friends, they have been both my critics as well as my supporters. Their diverse perspectives have enriched this book in many ways. "You guys rock!"

I'm thankful to my editor **Miss Arpita Biwal**, for her constant support. Her contributions have greatly enhanced this book from various angles. For this, and for the countless things, I am wholeheartedly grateful to her. "Thank you so much for your invaluable support, Arpita."

I acknowledge and am thankful for the diligent efforts provided by the editor, **Mrs Diti Shah**, for her support and editorial expertise. "I highly appreciate you, Diti."

Also, I extend my heartfelt thanks to every challenge that I faced in my life, and every setback that threatened to break my spirit. They were not mere obstacles, but profound teachers. "Without you, I wouldn't have learned to rise again."

And finally, to you, my dear reader. Thank you for embarking on this journey with me. I hope these stories made you laugh, cry, and feel inspired as they did to me.

With gratitude,

Sara

About Author

Saranya E M is an Indian author who discovered her true calling in the world of words during a successful career in IT. Sara then made a bold transition from the tech industry to writing when she realised the transformative power of shared knowledge and its potential to impact the world.

Her mission is straightforward yet profound—"Let's make evolution wiser together." She believes that by sharing our collective wisdom, we can help each other bypass life's struggles and move forward rapidly. This philosophy is at the heart of her debut book, **"The Secret Impacts"**. It encapsulates her experiences and the lessons learned from the commoners she met; all intertwined into compelling narratives to entertain and help readers to overcome challenges.

www.ingramcontent.com/pod-product-compliance
Lightning Source LLC
Chambersburg PA
CBHW031126130726
47988CB00006B/2240